Betty Crocker®
whole grains

WITH BONUS **QUINOA** RECIPES

WILEY

John Wiley & Sons, Inc.

What is Quinoa?

Ever wonder just what Quinoa is? Native to South America and a staple food of the Inca civilization, this tasty food is considered a whole grain even though it is actually a relative of leafy green vegetables like spinach and Swiss chard.

But regardless of its origins, the benefits of quinoa are numerous and include high protein content, many healthful nutrients plus fiber, and an added bonus—it cooks very quickly. So whether you are familiar with this versatile ancient grain or have never tried quinoa, you'll want to sample these recipes that showcase the mild, slightly nutty flavor it is known for.

Quinoa-Almond Salad

PREP TIME: **20 MINUTES** • START TO FINISH: **35 MINUTES** • **6 SERVINGS** •
WHOLE GRAIN SERVING: **1⅓**

Quinoa

1 cup uncooked quinoa

2 cups water

½ teaspoon salt

½ cup coarsely shredded
    carrot (about 1 small)

¼ cup sliced almonds, toasted*

¼ cup dried cherries
    or cranberries

Vinaigrette

2 tablespoons chopped
    fresh parsley

1½ tablespoons canola or
    soybean oil

2 tablespoons balsamic vinegar

½ teaspoon salt

Dash of pepper

✱ To toast almonds, bake uncovered in ungreased shallow pan in 350°F oven about 10 minutes, stirring occasionally, until golden brown. Or cook in ungreased heavy skillet over medium-low heat 5 to 7 minutes, stirring frequently until browning begins, then stirring constantly until golden brown.

1 Rinse quinoa thoroughly by placing in a fine mesh strainer and holding under cold running water until water runs clear; drain well.

2 In 2-quart saucepan, heat quinoa, water and salt to boiling, stirring once or twice. Reduce heat to low. Cover; simmer 12 to 15 minutes or until water is absorbed and quinoa is tender.

3 Remove saucepan from heat; let stand 5 minutes. Fluff quinoa with fork; cool 15 minutes.

4 In large bowl, beat vinaigrette ingredients with whisk until blended. Stir in quinoa and remaining ingredients. Serve warm, or cover and refrigerate about 4 hours or until chilled. If desired, serve on lettuce leaves.

Betty Tip

Adding toasted nuts to grains such as quinoa really brings out the flavor. Quinoa is higher in unsaturated (good) fats and protein and lower in carbohydrates than most grains so there are many reasons to include it in a healthy diet.

1 Serving: Calories 190 (Calories from Fat 60); Total Fat 7g (Saturated Fat 0.5g; Trans Fat 0g); Cholesterol 0mg; Sodium 410mg; Total Carbohydrate 26g (Dietary Fiber 3g; Sugars 8g); Protein 5g **% Daily Value:** Vitamin A 40%; Vitamin C 0%; Calcium 4%; Iron 10% **Exchanges:** 1 Starch, ½ Other Carbohydrate, 1½ Fat **Carbohydrate Choices:** 2

Quinoa and Corn Salad

Salad

½ cup uncooked quinoa

1 cup water

¾ cup frozen whole kernel corn

1 cucumber, peeled if desired

2 stalks celery, sliced (¾ cup)

½ medium red bell
    pepper, chopped

½ cup thinly sliced red onion

Dressing

2 tablespoons white
    wine vinegar

2 tablespoons fresh lime juice

1 clove garlic, finely chopped

1 teaspoon ground cumin

¼ teaspoon salt

¼ teaspoon pepper

¼ cup olive oil

2 tablespoons finely chopped
    fresh cilantro

1 Rinse quinoa thoroughly by placing in a fine mesh strainer and holding under cold running water until water runs clear; drain well.

2 In 1-quart saucepan, heat quinoa and 1 cup water to boiling. Reduce heat to low. Cover; simmer 15 to 20 minutes or until water is absorbed and quinoa is tender. Cool slightly. Meanwhile, cook corn as directed on package; cool.

3 Cut cucumber in half lengthwise; remove seeds and cut into 1½ × ¼-inch strips. In large bowl, stir cucumber, celery, bell pepper, onion, cooked quinoa and corn.

4 In small bowl, beat vinegar, lime juice, garlic, cumin, salt and pepper with whisk until blended. Beat in oil. Pour dressing over quinoa mixture; toss to coat. Sprinkle with cilantro.

Betty Tip

A lime will yield the maximum amount of juice if allowed to come to room temperature first. Roll the lime firmly on the counter, then cut in half and juice. Typically a lime will yield about 1 to 2 tablespoons of juice. For this recipe, choose a large lime so it will yield the amount of juice needed.

1 Serving: Calories 80 (Calories from Fat 45); Total Fat 5g (Saturated Fat 0.5g; Trans Fat 0g); Cholesterol 0mg; Sodium 55mg; Total Carbohydrate 8g (Dietary Fiber 1g; Sugars 1g); Protein 1g
% Daily Value: Vitamin A 4%; Vitamin C 6%; Calcium 0%; Iron 4% **Exchanges:** ½ Starch, 1 Fat
Carbohydrate Choices: ½

Quinoa Veggie Salad

PREP TIME: **15 MINUTES** • START TO FINISH: **35 MINUTES** • **3 SERVINGS (1 CUP EACH)** • WHOLE GRAIN SERVING: **2**

¾ cup uncooked quinoa

1½ cups water

1 cup torn arugula

¼ cup chopped roasted red bell peppers (from a jar)

¼ cup halved yellow or red cherry tomatoes

¼ cup chopped marinated artichokes

1 tablespoon marinade from marinated artichoke jar

1 tablespoon lemon juice

¼ teaspoon salt

¼ teaspoon pepper

1 Rinse quinoa thoroughly by placing in a fine mesh strainer and holding under cold running water until water runs clear; drain well. Cook quinoa in water as directed on package; cool.

2 In 2-quart saucepan, heat quinoa and water to boiling. Reduce heat to low. Cover; simmer 15 to 20 minutes or until water is absorbed and quinoa is tender.

3 In medium bowl, mix quinoa, arugula, roasted peppers, tomatoes and artichokes. Add remaining ingredients; mix well. Cover; refrigerate until serving time.

Betty Tip

If you've never tried arugula, you'll find that it adds a peppery, mustard-like flavor and bright green color to the salad. Look for arugula with other greens at the grocery store or at farmers' markets.

1 Serving: Calories 180 (Calories from Fat 30); Total Fat 3.5g (Saturated Fat 0.5g; Trans Fat 0g); Cholesterol 0mg; Sodium 290mg; Total Carbohydrate 31g (Dietary Fiber 5g; Sugars 4g); Protein 7g **% Daily Value:** Vitamin A 10%; Vitamin C 20%; Calcium 4%; Iron 15% **Exchanges:** 1½ Starch, 1 Vegetable, ½ Fat **Carbohydrate Choices:** 2

Summer Quinoa-Tomato Salad

PREP TIME: **15 MINUTES** • START TO FINISH: **35 MINUTES** • **8 SERVINGS** •
WHOLE GRAIN SERVING: ¾

¾ cup uncooked quinoa

1½ cups water

2 large tomatoes, quartered, cut into cubes

¼ medium red onion, chopped

2 cloves garlic, finely chopped

3 tablespoons chopped fresh basil leaves

3 tablespoons chopped fresh Italian (flat-leaf) parsley

1½ tablespoons olive oil

3 tablespoons balsamic vinegar

½ teaspoon salt

¼ teaspoon freshly ground black pepper

2 teaspoons sugar

¼ cup grated Parmesan cheese

1 Rinse quinoa thoroughly by placing in a fine mesh strainer and holding under cold running water until water runs clear; drain well.

2 In 2-quart saucepan, heat quinoa and water to boiling. Reduce heat to low. Cover; simmer 15 to 20 minutes or until water is absorbed and quinoa is tender. Cool slightly.

3 In medium bowl, toss tomatoes, onion, garlic, basil, parsley, oil, vinegar, salt, pepper and sugar.

4 Spread cooled cooked quinoa in large serving bowl or on platter; spoon tomato mixture over top. Cover; refrigerate until serving time. Just before serving, sprinkle with cheese.

Betty Tip

Get creative! Add a little feta cheese, olives, fresh chopped oregano, or other cheeses and herbs.

Blogger Arlene Cummings of cookingwithsugar.com shares a quinoa and tomato salad recipe. Quinoa is a super food and super easy to make. You will love the fresh taste of the tomatoes and basil in this refreshingly healthy dish.

1 Serving: Calories 110 (Calories from Fat 40); Total Fat 4.5g (Saturated Fat 1g; Trans Fat 0g); Cholesterol 0mg; Sodium 210mg; Total Carbohydrate 14g (Dietary Fiber 1g; Sugars 4g); Protein 4g **% Daily Value:** Vitamin A 10%; Vitamin C 15%; Calcium 6%; Iron 6% **Exchanges:** 1 Starch, 1 Fat **Carbohydrate Choices:** 1

Breakfast Quinoa

PREP TIME: **5 MINUTES** • START TO FINISH: **20 MINUTES** •
4 SERVINGS (½ CUP EACH) • WHOLE GRAIN SERVING: **2**

1 cup uncooked quinoa

2 cups water, milk or soymilk

¼ teaspoon ground cinnamon

1 cup fresh or frozen
   (thawed) blueberries

¼ cup pecans or walnuts,
   toasted if desired

Maple syrup, if desired

1 Rinse quinoa thoroughly by placing in a fine mesh strainer and holding under cold running water until water runs clear; drain well.

2 In 1-quart saucepan, heat quinoa and water to boiling. Reduce heat to low; cover and simmer 15 minutes or until liquid is absorbed (mixture will still be moist) and quinoa is tender.

3 Stir in cinnamon. Spoon quinoa into bowls. Top with blueberries and pecans. Sweeten to taste with a drizzle of maple syrup.

Betty Tip

Use more liquid for a creamier cereal, or serve additional milk or cream on the side.

Blogger Elizabeth Dehn from beautybets.com shares a favorite recipe. Quinoa makes a quick and hearty base for this new spin on hot cereal. Experiment with healthy mix-ins to make it your own.

1 Serving: Calories 230 (Calories from Fat 60); Total Fat 7g (Saturated Fat 0.5g; Trans Fat 0g); Cholesterol 0mg; Sodium 5mg; Total Carbohydrate 34g (Dietary Fiber 4g; Sugars 7g); Protein 7g **% Daily Value:** Vitamin A 0%; Vitamin C 4%; Calcium 4%; Iron 10% **Exchanges:** 2½ Starch, 1 Fat **Carbohydrate Choices:** 2

Quinoa with Color and Citrus

PREP TIME: **15 MINUTES** • START TO FINISH: **35 MINUTES** • **6 SERVINGS** • WHOLE GRAIN SERVING: **2**

Vinaigrette

2 to 3 tablespoons lime juice

2 to 3 tablespoons lemon juice

⅛ teaspoon white pepper

1 medium jalapeño chile, seeded, finely chopped

½ teaspoon coarse salt

¼ cup olive oil

Quinoa and Vegetables

1½ cups uncooked quinoa

3 cups water

½ cup diced, seeded, peeled cucumber

½ cup diced seeded tomato

½ cup coarsely chopped sweet bell pepper (red, yellow, orange)

¼ cup sliced green onions (white part only)

¼ cup chopped fresh Italian (flat-leaf) parsley

¼ cup chopped fresh mint leaves

Salt and freshly ground black pepper to taste

1 In small bowl, beat all vinaigrette ingredients with whisk until blended. Set aside.

2 Rinse quinoa thoroughly by placing in a fine mesh strainer and holding under cold running water until water runs clear; drain well.

3 In 4-quart saucepan, heat quinoa and water to boiling. Reduce heat to low. Cover; simmer about 10 minutes or until water is absorbed and quinoa is just tender. Do not overcook. Drain thoroughly. Let stand until cool, about 10 minutes.

4 In large bowl, toss quinoa with remaining ingredients and vinaigrette. Serve at room temperature or chilled.

Betty Tip

This is a really versatile salad—it's easy to add favorite veggies to suit your taste. Try adding a handful of sliced ripe olives, some shredded or chopped carrot or even some cooked corn kernels to the salad for a little change of flavor and color.

1 Serving: Calories 250 (Calories from Fat 110); Total Fat 12g (Saturated Fat 1.5g; Trans Fat 0g); Cholesterol 0mg; Sodium 200mg; Total Carbohydrate 30g (Dietary Fiber 4g; Sugars 4g); Protein 6g **% Daily Value:** Vitamin A 15%; Vitamin C 25%; Calcium 4%; Iron 15% **Exchanges:** 2 Starch, 2 Fat **Carbohydrate Choices:** 2

Italian Broccoli and Quinoa Pilaf

PREP TIME: **15 MINUTES** • START TO FINISH: **35 MINUTES** •
6 SERVINGS (²⁄₃ CUP EACH) • WHOLE GRAIN SERVING: **1¹⁄₃**

1 cup uncooked quinoa

1 tablespoon olive oil

¼ cup finely chopped onion

2 cloves garlic, finely chopped

¼ cup julienne-cut sun-dried tomatoes (not oil-packed)

½ teaspoon dried oregano leaves

¼ teaspoon salt

2 cups water

2 cups frozen broccoli florets

Shredded fresh Parmesan cheese, if desired

1 Rinse quinoa thoroughly by placing in a fine mesh strainer and holding under cold running water until water runs clear; drain well.

2 In 3-quart saucepan, heat oil over medium heat. Add onion and garlic; cook about 2 minutes or until onion is crisp-tender, stirring occasionally.

3 Add quinoa, sun-dried tomatoes, oregano, salt and water. Heat to boiling. Reduce heat to low. Cover; simmer 8 minutes. Uncover; stir in broccoli. Cover; cook 7 to 8 minutes longer or until water is absorbed and broccoli and quinoa are tender.

4 To serve, sprinkle with Parmesan cheese.

Betty Tip

Quinoa, an ancient grain, is indeed a whole grain. Eating at least 3 servings of whole grain daily may help reduce blood cholesterol.

1 Serving: Calories 150 (Calories from Fat 35); Total Fat 4g (Saturated Fat 0.5g; Trans Fat 0g); Cholesterol 0mg; Sodium 160mg; Total Carbohydrate 23g (Dietary Fiber 4g; Sugars 4g); Protein 6g **% Daily Value:** Vitamin A 10%; Vitamin C 15%; Calcium 4%; Iron 10% **Exchanges:** 1½ Starch, ½ Vegetable, ½ Fat **Carbohydrate Choices:** 1½

Quinoa with Black Beans

PREP TIME: **15 MINUTES** • START TO FINISH: **35 MINUTES** • **8 SERVINGS (½ CUP EACH)** • WHOLE GRAIN SERVING: **1**

1 cup uncooked quinoa

2 cups chicken broth
(from 32-oz carton)

1 cup black beans (from 15-oz
can), drained, rinsed

½ cup frozen whole kernel
corn, thawed

1 small tomato, chopped
(½ cup)

¼ cup chopped fresh cilantro

4 medium green onions,
chopped (¼ cup)

1 tablespoon fresh lime juice

1 clove garlic, finely chopped

¼ teaspoon salt

1 Rinse quinoa thoroughly by placing in a fine mesh strainer and holding under cold running water until water runs clear; drain well.

2 In 2-quart saucepan, heat broth to boiling. Add quinoa; reduce heat to low. Cover; simmer 15 to 20 minutes or until liquid is absorbed and quinoa is tender.

3 Fluff quinoa with fork. Stir in remaining ingredients. Cook uncovered about 3 minutes, stirring occasionally, until thoroughly heated.

Betty Tip

Quinoa is high in protein, low in fat and cooks quickly, making it a great grain to use often.

1 Serving: Calories 260 (Calories from Fat 30); Total Fat 3g (Saturated Fat 0g; Trans Fat 0g); Cholesterol 0mg; Sodium 740mg; Total Carbohydrate 45g (Dietary Fiber 8g; Sugars 5g); Protein 12g **% Daily Value:** Vitamin A 10%; Vitamin C 8%; Calcium 6%; Iron 20% **Exchanges:** 2½ Starch, 1½ Vegetable, ½ Fat **Carbohydrate Choices:** 3

Southwestern Quinoa

PREP TIME: **10 MINUTES** • START TO FINISH: **2 HOURS 50 MINUTES** • **8 SERVINGS (¾ CUP EACH)** • WHOLE GRAIN SERVING: **1½**

1½ cups uncooked quinoa

1 tablespoon vegetable oil

2 large onions, chopped (2 cups)

½ teaspoon salt

½ teaspoon dried oregano leaves

3 cups chicken broth (from 32-oz carton)

1 can (15 oz) spicy chili beans, undrained

1 jar (7 oz) roasted red bell peppers, drained, chopped (¾ cup)

¼ cup chopped fresh cilantro

1 Rinse quinoa thoroughly by placing in a fine mesh strainer and holding under cold running water until water runs clear; drain well.

2 In 10-inch skillet, heat oil over medium heat. Add onions and cook about 5 minutes, stirring occasionally, until tender.

3 Spray 3- to 4-quart slow cooker with cooking spray. In slow cooker, mix onions, quinoa, salt, oregano, broth and beans. Cover; cook on Low heat setting 2 hours 30 minutes to 3 hours 30 minutes.

4 With large fork, gently stir roasted peppers into mixture in slow cooker. Cover; cook 10 minutes longer or until thoroughly heated. Stir in cilantro.

Betty Tip

Substitute sun-dried tomatoes for the roasted red bell peppers. Choose sun-dried tomatoes in oil and herbs for even more flavor. Drain and chop enough to get ¾ cup. Any leftover oil from the tomatoes can be the start to a tasty salad dressing. Simply follow a recipe for a vinaigrette, using the leftover oil for the oil called for in the recipe.

1 Serving: Calories 220 (Calories from Fat 45); Total Fat 5g (Saturated Fat 0.5g; Trans Fat 0g); Cholesterol 0mg; Sodium 920mg; Total Carbohydrate 35g (Dietary Fiber 5g; Sugars 7g); Protein 9g **% Daily Value:** Vitamin A 15%; Vitamin C 35%; Calcium 4%; Iron 15% **Exchanges:** 1½ Starch, ½ Other Carbohydrate, 1 Vegetable, 1 Fat **Carbohydrate Choices:** 2

Citrus Pork Tenderloin with Ginger Quinoa

PREP TIME: **20 MINUTES**   •   START TO FINISH: **1 HOUR 20 MINUTES**   •   **4 SERVINGS**   •   WHOLE GRAIN SERVING: **2**

Pork and Marinade

1 pork tenderloin (about 1 lb)

3 tablespoons olive oil

2 tablespoons lemon juice

1 tablespoon grated
    orange peel

1 teaspoon grated
    fresh gingerroot

¼ teaspoon ground cumin

¼ teaspoon salt

1 clove garlic, finely chopped

Quinoa

1 cup uncooked quinoa

1 tablespoon butter
    or margarine

¼ cup chopped green onions
    (4 medium)

2 cups orange juice

2 teaspoons grated
    fresh gingerroot

¼ teaspoon salt

½ cup dried currants

1 tablespoon chopped fresh
    mint leaves

1   Place pork and marinade ingredients in large resealable plastic food-storage bag. Refrigerate 30 minutes to blend flavors.

2   Heat oven to 400°F. Place pork on rack in shallow pan; reserve marinade. Bake pork 35 to 45 minutes, spooning marinade over pork occasionally, until meat thermometer inserted in center reads 145°F. Cover; let stand at least 3 minutes before serving.

3   Meanwhile, rinse quinoa thoroughly by placing in a fine mesh strainer and holding under cold running water until water runs clear; drain well.

4   In 2-quart saucepan, melt butter over medium heat. Add quinoa and onions; cook about 2 minutes or until quinoa and onions are lightly toasted. Stir in orange juice, 2 teaspoons gingerroot and ¼ teaspoon salt. Heat to boiling. Reduce heat to low. Cover; simmer 15 to 20 minutes or until liquid is absorbed and quinoa is tender. Stir in currants.

5   Cut pork tenderloin into thin slices. Spoon quinoa onto serving platter; top with pork slices. Sprinkle with mint.

1 Serving: Calories 530 (Calories from Fat 180); Total Fat 20g (Saturated Fat 5g; Trans Fat 0g); Cholesterol 55mg; Sodium 380mg; Total Carbohydrate 57g (Dietary Fiber 5g; Sugars 26g); Protein 30g **% Daily Value:** Vitamin A 4%; Vitamin C 40%; Calcium 6%; Iron 20% **Exchanges:** 3 Starch, 1 Fruit, 1½ Very Lean Meat, 1½ Lean Meat, 2½ Fat **Carbohydrate Choices:** 4

Betty Crocker

whole grains

easy everyday recipes

WILEY

John Wiley & Sons, Inc.

General Mills

Publisher, Cookbooks: Maggie Gilbert, Lynn Vettel
Manager, Cookbook Publishing: Lois Tlusty
Senior Editor: Cheri Olerud and Grace Wells
Recipe Development and Testing: Betty Crocker Kitchens
Photography and Food Styling: General Mills Photography Studios and Image Library
Photographer: Dennis Becker (Interior)
Photographer: Val Bourassa (Cover)
Food Stylists: Cindy Syme and Sue Brue
Nutritionists: Suzanne Skapyak, M.S., R.D. and Margaret Reinhart, MPH, LN

John Wiley & Sons, Inc.

Publisher: Natalie Chapman
Associate Publisher: Jessica Goodman
Executive Editor: Anne Ficklen
Senior Editorial Assistant: Charleen Barila and Heather Dabah
Senior Production Editor: Jacqueline Beach
Cover Design: Suzanne Sunwoo
Art Director: Tai Blanche
Interior Design and Layout: Holly Wittenberg
Manufacturing Manager: Kevin Watt

The Betty Crocker Kitchens seal guarantees success in your kitchen. Every recipe has been tested in America's Most Trusted Kitchens™ to meet our high standards of reliability, easy preparation and great taste.

FIND MORE GREAT IDEAS AT
BettyCrocker.com

Dear Friends,

Of course you've heard about whole grains, but maybe you haven't discovered how truly amazing they are. Perhaps you're not sure if they taste good, or just how important they are in your diet. If you're exploring new territory, this cookbook will show you how easy and fun whole grains can be in your family's favorite meals. With Pizza Burgers, Mixed-Berry Coffeecake and Baked Apple Oatmeal using whole grains will be an easy—and a tasty—change.

Maybe you already know how delicious grains are, and you're looking for more great grain recipes. If you're a whole grain fan, you'll enjoy the extra flavor, hardy texture and endless variety they add to your recipes. Here, you'll find many new ways to use the grains you love, like Three-Seed Flatbread, Asian Stir-Fry with Millet and Rye Berry Borscht.

Though whole grains have been in the limelight recently, grains have actually been around for centuries. Quinoa was a key grain in the Inca culture, wheat was growing in Europe in the 1700s and corn was being harvested by Native Americans long before Europeans came to America.

In this cookbook, you'll find the latest and greatest information on buying whole grains, how to cook and what to pair with them. With this family-friendly resource, you'll be able to easily go with the grain!

Warmly,

Betty Crocker

Contents

unraveling the mystery of whole grains

Quinoa, kasha, bulgur, wheat berries…
what are these mystery foods? Though the
names may sound mysterious, grains are
really quite simple and easy to cook. Their
wholesome appearance, chewy texture and
nutty, hearty flavor make them delicious
and enjoyable for lunch, dinner, snacks
and desserts. Check out the
answers to the top questions
about whole grains:

Q. What is a whole grain?

A. A whole grain is the entire seed of a grass plant and contains all parts of the grain kernel: the fiber-rich outer coating of **bran**; the energy-dense middle layer, called the **endosperm**; and the nutrient-packed **germ**. The wheat kernel, shown here, describes each part of the grain and what it contains.

The kernel of the grain can either be cracked, crushed or flaked and still be considered a whole grain as long as it contains the same balance of each part of the whole kernel. If any part of the grain has been removed and discarded, like the bran or the germ, it's no longer considered a whole grain.

What's so great about whole grains is that because all parts of the grain are included, so are all of the nutrients from part of the grain. A whole grain contains a whole package of healthy nutrients, like essential vitamins and minerals, healthy fats, antioxidants and phytonutrients.

Q. What's the difference between whole grains and fiber?

A. Whole grains and fiber are not the same. Whole grains naturally contain fiber in the outer coating of the grain kernel, the bran. Fiber is a component of whole grains, but there are many other important nutrients and natural compounds found in whole grains that work together to provide health benefits. Eating whole grains can be a helpful way to get more fiber, but not all whole grains are high in fiber. Eating plenty of fruits, vegetables, beans and legumes in addition to whole grains will help you get the fiber you need.

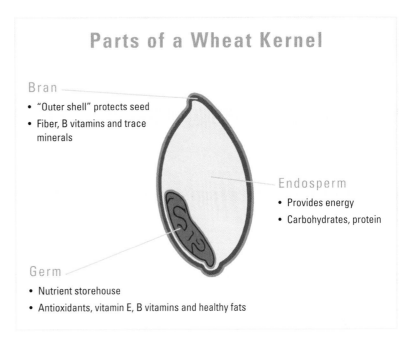

Parts of a Wheat Kernel

Bran
- "Outer shell" protects seed
- Fiber, B vitamins and trace minerals

Endosperm
- Provides energy
- Carbohydrates, protein

Germ
- Nutrient storehouse
- Antioxidants, vitamin E, B vitamins and healthy fats

know your grains

AMARANTH

HULLED BARLEY

ROLLED BARLEY

BROWN RICE

BUCKWHEAT

YELLOW WHOLE-GRAIN CORNMEAL

KAMUT®   *Kamut® is a registered trademark of Kamut International Ltd.*

MILLET

OLD-FASHIONED OATS

STEEL-CUT OATS

OAT GROATS

RYE BERRIES

GOLD QUINOA

ROLLED RYE FLAKES

RED QUINOA

SPELT

IVORY TEFF

BULGUR WHEAT

WHEAT BERRIES

WILD RICE

Q. Which grains are considered whole?

A. Whole grains include:

Amaranth	Kamut®	Sorghum
Barley (hulled, rolled and lightly pearled)	Millet	Spelt
Brown rice	Oats (oat groats, steel-cut, old-fashioned and quick-cooking)	Teff
Buckwheat (also known as kasha; includes buckwheat flour)	Quinoa (gold and red)	Wheat (wheat berries, bulgur wheat, cracked wheat and whole wheat flour)
Corn (includes whole cornmeal, popcorn and tortilla chips)	Rye (rye berries, rolled rye flakes and whole rye flour)	Wild rice

Recipes for most of these grains are included in this cookbook. Recipes for amaranth, Kamut®, sorghum, spelt, teff and triticale are not included because these grains are not very common and are often difficult to find in typical supermarkets. Some of the recipes in this cookbook also use cereals made from whole grains. Adding whole grains may be as simple as using what's in your pantry, but check the label for the words "whole grain" to be sure.

Q. Where do I find whole grains?

A. You can get whole grains either as an individual food, like brown rice or oatmeal, or in whole-grain products, like breads, pastas and cereals. Hunting for certain grains can be a bit of a challenge. Look in supermarkets (sometimes in the bulk-foods section), organic markets and natural- or health-food stores. Don't be discouraged or give up if you don't find a certain whole grain right away; talk to the store manager about stocking the items you'd like to try.

Quite a variety of grains can be purchased on the Internet. The following are Web sites where you can purchase whole grains online:

Bob's Red Mill at www.bobsredmill.com

What's a serving of whole grain? One serving equals:

1 slice of 100% whole wheat or whole-grain bread

1/2 of a 100% whole-grain English muffin

1/2 cup cooked brown rice, barley or other whole grain

1/2 cup cooked 100% whole grain cereal

3 cups of popped popcorn

1/2 cup of a 100% whole wheat pasta

Gold Mine Natural Food Co. at www.goldminenaturalfood.com

Hodgson Mill at www.hodgsonmill.com

Kalustyan's at www.kalustyans.com

Q. How do I know if a product is a whole grain?

A. Identifying whole grains may be a mystery, but the best way to determine whether a product is whole grain is to read the label. There are three things you can look for—the words "whole" or "whole grain" before a grain's name in the ingredient list or a "Whole Grain" seal or logo or check for the whole grain health claim. The whole grain seals and logos may be included on the package of some whole grain foods. The Whole Grain Council, a nonprofit industry group, developed stamps to help consumers identify foods that provide a nutritionally significant amount of whole grain; at least 8 grams per serving. The Whole Grains Council has two different stamps that food manufacturers can use, one on products that provide at least 8 grams of whole grain and the other is the 100% Whole Grain Stamp for products that use only whole grains and provide at least 16 grams of whole grain per serving.

Grain Words

For more, visit the Whole Grain Council at www.wholegrainscouncil.org.

Q. How do I store whole grains?

A. Because whole grains contain all parts of the kernel (the germ contains the beneficial grain fat), they will not keep quite as long as refined grain flours. Depending on how quickly you use them, it's best to

THESE WORDS ON A PACKAGE:	MEAN THIS:
Whole grain, Whole wheat, Whole (other grain), Stone-ground whole (grain), Brown rice	It is whole grain. It contains all parts of the grain, so you'll get all the nutrients of the whole grain.
Wheat flour, Durum wheat, Organic flour, Multigrain (may describe several refined grains or a mix of both), Seven-grain	May not be a whole grain. Because some parts of the grain might be missing, you might be missing the whole-grain benefits.
Unbleached flour, Enriched flour Bran, Wheat flour, Wheat germ, Semolina, Degerminated (corn)	Not whole grain. It contains only parts of the grain.

Look for these stamps:

Look for this health claim:

Foods containing a high percentage of whole grains can make the following claim on their labels: "Diets rich in whole-grain foods and other plant foods that are low in total fat, saturated fat and cholesterol may reduce the risk of heart disease and certain cancers."

store whole-grain flours in the refrigerator for up to six months, or freeze for longer storage, up to one year. Most other whole grains, like hulled or lightly pearled barley, millet, quinoa, oats and brown rice, can be kept in an airtight container in a cool, dry place and will stay fresh that way for several months.

Q. How much whole grain do I need to eat?

A. Because whole grains contribute fiber and other nutrients, the (published jointly by the Department of Health and Human Services and the Department of Agriculture) suggest that adults eat half of their grains as whole grains. That's at least three servings (or a minimum of 48 grams) of whole grain every day. Capture the goodness of whole grains by eating a variety of grains.

In this cookbook, look for the number of whole-grain servings listed in either one-half servings (equal to 8 grams) or whole servings (equal to 16 grams) under the title of each recipe. This will help you determine how you can get up to three servings (48 grams) or more every day.

eating whole grains
every day

For more on eating three servings of whole grains each day, check out "Finding Your Way to a Healthier You" at www.health.gov/dietaryguidelines and "Steps to a Healthier You" at www.choosemyplate.gov. Once you start to keep track, you'll see that it really isn't hard to get three servings of whole grains each day. See the two examples on the next page to get started:

3 Servings of Whole Grains from Ready-to-Eat Foods

BREAKFAST

1 cup cereal made from whole grains, such as Cheerios® =
1 whole-grain serving

LUNCH OR DINNER

1 sandwich made with 2 slices 100% whole wheat bread =
2 whole-grain servings

Daily total: 3 whole-grain servings

3 Servings of Whole Grains from Recipes

BREAKFAST

1 serving Baked Apple Oatmeal (page 34) =
1½ whole-grain servings

DINNER

1 serving Italian Frittata with Vinaigrette Tomatoes (page 112)
= ½ whole-grain serving

or

1 cup Vegetable-Beef-Barley Soup (page 157)
and 1 Hearty Three-Grain Biscuit (page 163) =
1 whole-grain serving

SNACK

1 serving Campfire Popcorn Snack (page 84) =
½ whole-grain serving

Daily total: 3½ whole-grain servings

Q. How do I start adding whole grains to my meals?

A. Whole grains add texture and eye appeal to any recipe or dish. If you're not familiar with whole grains, starting may be a bit daunting because there are so many choices. To begin, try the following:

- Buy 100% whole wheat or whole-grain breads and buns.
- Eat whole-grain cereals, pasta, tortillas and crackers whose first ingredient is "whole wheat" or "whole grain."
- Try whole wheat couscous in place of regular couscous. The kids won't even know the difference.
- Enjoy 100% whole wheat bagels, English muffins, pita breads and whole wheat or corn tortillas.
- Eat hot whole-grains, like oatmeal, for breakfast. If you like variety, there are many interesting new hot whole-grain cereal combinations to try. To be certain they are whole grain, look for whole grain in the ingredient list.

- Eat ready-to-eat cereals made from whole grain for breakfast or snacks. Cheerios®, Wheaties®, Oatmeal Crisp® Raisin, Total®, Fiber One® and Wheat Chex® are cereals that provide 1 serving of whole grain.

- Transition into whole grains. If your family isn't ready to go all the way to whole wheat pasta, start with a combination of regular and whole wheat pasta until they are used to the combination. Once they like it, use all whole wheat pasta.

- Try ethnic dishes with interesting grains, like quinoa from South America or bulgur wheat in tabbouleh from the Middle East.

- Add ½ cup already-cooked bulgur wheat, wild rice or hulled barley to stuffing.

- Add ½ cup cooked wheat or rye berries, brown rice, wild rice or hulled barley to your favorite soups.

- Make snack mixes and treats using ready-to-eat cereals made with whole grain and popcorn, along with other ingredients like nuts, dried fruits and chocolate chips. (See Chapter 3, Grains on the Go.)

- Choose whole grains over refined grains (brown rice that contains the bran instead of white rice that has the bran removed), hulled barley over pearled barley (the bran is removed in the pearling process).

- Use whole wheat flour for half of the all-purpose flour called for when baking breads, muffins, pancakes, biscuits, waffles and cookies. If you like the results, next time try all whole wheat flour in place of the all-purpose flour. (Whole-grain breads will usually be heavier.)

- Experiment with less-common but also nutritious whole grains, like quinoa, millet, rye berries, wheat berries and kasha, for variety.

Q. How do I cook whole grains?

A. In the kitchen, you'll find that grains are actually easy to cook, very versatile and a lot of fun to experiment with. When cooking grains, follow these easy tips:

Find a heavy pan: Use a heavy-bottomed pot with a tight-fitting lid. To determine if the pot is large enough, dump the grains in the pot; if the grains are more than 1½ inches deep, switch to a larger pot.

To add a little flavor: Add ½ teaspoon to 1 teaspoon salt, if desired, to the cooking water. Also see Flavor Boosters, page 17.

A couple of notes about cooking whole grains:

Cook only for the time designated. You may notice that the texture is more chewy than you're used to. That's natural with whole grains, and that's what people love about them. (Remember, you're chewing through the bran, endosperm and hull.)

Use only the amount of water recommended. If not all of the water is absorbed after the cooking time, cook 5 minutes longer; or if the grain is not done, add ¼ cup more water and cook 5 minutes longer. Do not drain; you're rinsing away valuable nutrients.

Cooking Whole Grains

GRAIN (1 CUP UNCOOKED)	WATER AMOUNT	SIMMER TIME (AFTER FIRST HEATING TO BOILING THEN REDUCING HEAT)	YIELD
Amaranth	5 cups	20 minutes	2 cups
Barley, hulled*	3½ cups	1 hour	4 cups
Brown Rice	2½ cups	45 to 50 minutes	3 cups
Buckwheat (Kasha)	2 cups	12 to 15 minutes	3 cups
Kamut®	2 quarts	1 to 1½ hours	3 cups
Millet	2½ cups	15 to 20 minutes	2½ cups
Oats, steel-cut	3 cups	15 to 20 minutes	2 cups
Quinoa	2 cups	12 to 15 minutes	3 cups
Rye Berries*	4 cups	50 to 60 minutes	3 cups
Sorghum	2 quarts	1 hour	2½ cups
Spelt	2 quarts	1½ to 2 hours	3 cups
Teff	3 cups	20 minutes	3 cups
Wheat berries*	1 quart	50 to 60 minutes	2 cups
Bulgur wheat	1½ cups	15 minutes	2 to 2½ cups
Wild Rice	2 cups	45 minutes	3 cups

Cook on low: Heat the water to boiling, cover the pan, then reduce heat to a bare simmer. If a bit of steam escapes, the heat is too high.

Keep a lid on it: Simmer with the lid on, and start checking to see if the grain is done only near the end of cooking. Each time you remove the lid, you release moisture, and the grains may turn out crunchy.

Give it a rest: Letting the grains stand, covered, for 5 to 10 minutes, which allows the cooked grain to firm up; fluff with a fork just before serving.

Cook extra: When cooking grains, cook extra to toss into soups, stews and chili (hulled barley, brown rice and bulgur wheat are good choices). Store cooked grains in an airtight container up to three days in the refrigerator, or freeze for up to six months.

Check the package: If you've purchased a grain that has directions on the package, follow them. If there are no package directions, consult the handy chart above to cook grains.

Flavor Boosters

Some grains are very flavorful on their own; others can be a bit more bland. To add more flavor to grains, try these suggestions:

Cooking Liquid—Raw grains are often cooked in water. To infuse flavor into wheat berries, hulled barley, bulgur wheat, millet or quinoa, instead of using water, cook in:

- Beef, chicken, turkey or vegetable broth
- Apple juice, orange juice or other juice blends
- Wine or half wine and half water
- Clam, tomato or vegetable juices

Toasting Grains—You may be familiar with the heightened flavor and texture of toasted nuts. You can do the same thing with grains before you cook them. Amaranth, millet, oats, quinoa and wheat berries can be toasted. The toasting time for each grain varies; watch closely so it doesn't get too dark.

- **In the Skillet:** Sprinkle up to ½ cup grain in ungreased heavy skillet. Cook over medium heat 3 to 7 minutes, stirring frequently until the grain begins to brown, then stirring constantly until golden brown.

- **In the Oven:** Heat oven to 350°F. Place up to ½ cup grain in ungreased shallow pan. Bake 5 to 10 minutes, stirring occasionally, until golden brown.

- **In the Microwave:** Place up to ½ cup grain in microwavable pie plate. Microwave on High 2 minutes 30 seconds to 3 minutes, stirring every 30 seconds, until light brown. If you use less than ½ cup grain, cooking times will be reduced; microwave in 30-second intervals until light brown.

Popcorn... a secret worth knowing about!

Pop quiz…what favorite movie goer's treat is considered a whole grain? If you guessed popcorn, you're right! Not only does it provide all the benefits of whole grain, but also it's a great low-fat snack that you can eat lots of—3 cups is one serving! (Just watch out for added calories from toppings.) Microwavable popcorn with zero trans fats and less than 1 gram saturated fat is a sensational snack and a great whole grain!

whole grain health benefits

Whole grains have received a lot of attention lately for their health benefits. Each grain varies a bit in its exact nutrient composition, but all provide essential vitamins and minerals like vitamin B-6, iron, zinc and magnesium as well as healthy fats and phytonutrients. In addition, whole grains are one of the richest sources of antioxidants and phytonutrients, natural plant compounds that work together to help keep you healthy.

From the Doctors

Q. Can eating whole grains help prevent disease?

A. Recent research shows that whole grains play an important role in overall good health. Eating whole grains as part of a healthy diet can help reduce the risk of heart disease and certain cancers, and may also help you maintain a healthy body weight. One area of promising research is the role whole grains may play in helping reduce the risk of diabetes. Read what general practice, heart, diabetes and cancer doctors, each a specialist in his or her own area, recommend to their patients regarding whole grains.

1. Whole Grains and Overall Good Health

Because whole grains contribute fiber, antioxidants and other nutrients, eating whole grains may help maintain overall good health and nutrition.

"So many of my patients ask about what to eat for good health. My answer: Whole grains, vegetables, fruits and protein that is low in saturated fat." Julia Halberg, M.D., M.S., M.P.H., Vice President Global Health & Chief Medical Officer for General Mills, Minneapolis, MN

"The link between diet and health continues to grow stronger with each new study published. The information is clear—eating whole grains is an important part of disease prevention." Julia Halberg, M.D., M.S., M.P.H., Vice President Global Health & Chief Medical Officer for General Mills, Minneapolis, MN

2. Whole Grains and Diabetes

Recent studies suggest that eating more whole grains may help reduce the risk of type 2 diabetes. The American Diabetes Association recommends including whole grains as part of a healthy diet.

"Managing weight is important for successfully managing diabetes. Studies show that diets rich in whole-grain foods can help you maintain a healthier body weight." Richard M. Bergenstal, M.D., Endocrinologist and Executive Director of the International Diabetes Center, St. Louis Park, MN

3. Whole Grains and Heart Health

A research study in the Journal of the American Medical Association, suggests that eating three servings of whole grains a day may reduce the risk of heart disease and stroke.

" Studies show that regularly consuming soluble fiber-rich foods, such as ready-to-eat whole-grain oat cereal, oatmeal or barley, may help reduce blood cholesterol levels, a leading risk factor for heart disease. "

Roger S. Blumenthal, M.D., Cardiologist and Director of The Johns Hopkins Ciccarone Center for the Prevention of Heart Disease, Baltimore, MD

4. Whole Grains and Weight Loss and Control

Whole grains can help you control your weight. Eating just three servings of whole grains daily may help you maintain a healthy body weight as you age.

" Whole grains have been shown to have an important impact on weight management. People who eat whole grains regularly have a lower risk of obesity, tend to weigh less and gain less weight over time than those who don't eat whole grains. " Susan J. Crockett, Ph.D., R.D., FADA, and Vice President, The Bell Institute of Health and Nutrition, General Mills, Minneapolis, MN

" In my work with families, parents are the role models of the family team. Since eating habits are formed in the early childhood years, parents can coach the kids and make whole grains a part of the family's lifestyle by:
- Introducing whole grains into children's diets when they start eating table foods, with whole-grain cereals, bread and crackers
- Making whole-grain foods part of family meals and snacks. "

James O. Hill, Ph.D., Professor of Pediatrics and a member of the Expert Panel on Obesity of the National Institutes of Health, Bethesda, MD

5. Whole Grains and Cancer Prevention

Studies show that diets rich in whole grains and other plant foods, and low in total fat, saturated fat and cholesterol, may reduce the risk of some cancers.

" Sound nutrition is perhaps the most important key to cancer prevention. Studies show that the antioxidants in whole grains may be beneficial in preventing some types of cancers. " Kris Ghosh, M.D., Gynecologic Oncologist, University of Southern California, Los Angeles

" Recent studies show that when eaten with fruits and vegetables, whole grains may play a strong role in preventing colo-rectal cancer. " Linda Carson, M.D., Gynecologic Oncologist, University of Minnesota, St. Paul, MN

better breakfasts

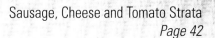

Sausage, Cheese and Tomato Strata
Page 42

1

Whole Wheat Waffles
with Honey–Peanut Butter Drizzle

PREP TIME: **35 MINUTES** • START TO FINISH: **35 MINUTES** • **8 SERVINGS** • WHOLE GRAIN SERVING: **1**

Waffles

2 eggs

1 cup whole wheat flour

1 cup all-purpose flour

2 cups buttermilk

1 tablespoon sugar

3 tablespoons canola oil

2 teaspoons baking powder

¼ teaspoon salt

½ cup low-fat granola

Drizzle

½ cup honey

¼ cup creamy peanut butter

1 Heat waffle iron. (Waffle irons without a nonstick coating may need to be brushed with canola oil or sprayed with cooking spray.) In medium bowl, beat eggs with fork or wire whisk until foamy. Beat in remaining waffle ingredients except granola just until smooth.

2 Pour batter from cup or pitcher onto center of hot waffle iron. (Check manufacturer's directions for recommended amount of batter.) Close lid of waffle iron.

3 Bake about 5 minutes or until steaming stops. Carefully remove waffle. Repeat with remaining batter.

4 Meanwhile, in small microwavable bowl, mix honey and peanut butter. Microwave uncovered on High 40 to 60 seconds or until warm; stir until smooth. Top each serving (2 waffle squares) with 1½ tablespoons honey mixture and 1 tablespoon granola.

Betty Tip

Besides being low in fat because it's made with skim milk, butter-milk is a powerful ingredient in baking because it adds a terrific dairy flavor and provides moistness. You'll love these easy waffles!

1 Serving: Calories 350 (Calories from Fat 110); Total Fat 12g (Saturated Fat 2g; Trans Fat 0g); Cholesterol 55mg; Sodium 330mg; Total Carbohydrate 52g (Dietary Fiber 3g; Sugars 25g); Protein 10g % Daily Value: Vitamin A 4%; Vitamin C 0%; Calcium 15%; Iron 10% **Exchanges:** 1½ Starch, 2 Other Carbohydrate, ½ High-Fat Meat, 1½ Fat **Carbohydrate Choices:** 3½

Nutty Silver Dollar Pancakes

PREP TIME: **25 MINUTES** • START TO FINISH: **25 MINUTES** • **6 SERVINGS** • WHOLE GRAIN SERVING: ½

2¼ cups Wheaties® cereal

¼ cup raisins

¼ cup dry-roasted sunflower nuts

2 cups Original Bisquick® mix

1¼ cups milk

2 eggs

⅓ cup vanilla low-fat yogurt

1 Place ¾ cup of the cereal in resealable food-storage plastic bag or between sheets of waxed paper; slightly crush with rolling pin. In small bowl, toss slightly crushed cereal (about ½ cup), the raisins and nuts; set aside.

2 Place remaining 1½ cups cereal in resealable food-storage plastic bag or between sheets of waxed paper; crush with rolling pin (will be about ¾ cup crushed).

3 Heat griddle to 375°F or heat 12-inch skillet over medium heat. Grease with canola oil if necessary (or spray with cooking spray before heating).

4 In medium bowl, stir Bisquick mix, ¾ cup crushed cereal, the milk and eggs with fork until blended. For each pancake, pour 1 measuring tablespoon batter onto hot griddle. Cook until edges are dry. Turn; cook other sides until golden.

5 For each serving, arrange 6 pancakes on plate. Top with 1 tablespoon yogurt and 2½ tablespoons cereal mixture.

Betty Tip

Take your pick of yogurt flavors to use on these good-for-you breakfast cakes.

1 Serving: Calories 330 (Calories from Fat 100); Total Fat 11g (Saturated Fat 3g; Trans Fat 1g); Cholesterol 75mg; Sodium 760mg; Total Carbohydrate 46g (Dietary Fiber 3g; Sugars 13g); Protein 10g **% Daily Value:** Vitamin A 10%; Vitamin C 2%; Calcium 20%; Iron 30% **Exchanges:** 3 Starch, 2 Fat **Carbohydrate Choices:** 3

Buckwheat Pancakes with Butter-Pecan Syrup

PREP TIME: **25 MINUTES** • START TO FINISH: **25 MINUTES** • **5 SERVINGS** • WHOLE GRAIN SERVING: **1½**

Syrup

1 tablespoon butter or
    margarine
3 tablespoons chopped pecans
½ cup maple-flavored syrup

Pancakes

1 egg
½ cup buckwheat flour
½ cup whole wheat flour
1 cup milk
1 tablespoon sugar
2 tablespoons canola oil
3 teaspoons baking powder
½ teaspoon salt
Whole bran or wheat germ,
    if desired

1 In 1-quart saucepan, melt butter over medium heat. Cook pecans in butter, stirring frequently, until browned. Stir in syrup; heat until hot. Remove from heat; keep warm.

2 Heat griddle to 375°F or heat 12-inch skillet over medium heat. Grease with canola oil if necessary (or spray with cooking spray before heating).

3 In medium bowl, beat egg with egg beater or wire whisk until fluffy. Beat in remaining pancake ingredients except bran just until smooth. For each pancake, pour about 3 tablespoons batter from cup or pitcher onto hot griddle. Cook pancakes until puffed and dry around edges. Sprinkle each pancake with 1 teaspoon bran. Turn; cook other sides until golden brown.

4 Top each serving (2 pancakes) with about 2 tablespoons syrup.

Betty Tip

Combining two whole grains, buckwheat flour and whole wheat flour, boosts the amount of whole grains in these delicious pancakes.

1 Serving: Calories 340 (Calories from Fat 120); Total Fat 13g (Saturated Fat 3g; Trans Fat 0g); Cholesterol 50mg; Sodium 620mg; Total Carbohydrate 48g (Dietary Fiber 3g; Sugars 17g); Protein 6g **% Daily Value:** Vitamin A 4%; Vitamin C 0%; Calcium 25%; Iron 8% **Exchanges:** 2 Starch, 1 Other Carbohydrate, 2½ Fat **Carbohydrate Choices:** 3

Whole-Grain Strawberry Pancakes

PREP TIME: **30 MINUTES** • START TO FINISH: **30 MINUTES** • **7 SERVINGS** • WHOLE GRAIN SERVING: **1½**

1½ cups whole wheat flour

3 tablespoons sugar

1 teaspoon baking powder

½ teaspoon baking soda

½ teaspoon salt

3 eggs

1 container (6 oz) vanilla
    low-fat yogurt

¾ cup water

3 tablespoons canola oil

1¾ cups sliced fresh
    strawberries

1 container (6 oz) strawberry
    low-fat yogurt

1 Heat griddle to 375°F or heat 12-inch skillet over medium heat. Grease with canola oil if necessary (or spray with cooking spray before heating).

2 In large bowl, mix flour, sugar, baking powder, baking soda and salt; set aside. In medium bowl, beat eggs, vanilla yogurt, water and oil with egg beater or wire whisk until well blended. Pour egg mixture all at once into flour mixture; stir until moistened.

3 For each pancake, pour slightly less than ¼ cup batter from cup or pitcher onto hot griddle. Cook pancakes 1 to 2 minutes or until bubbly on top, puffed and dry around edges. Turn; cook other sides 1 to 2 minutes or until golden brown.

4 Top each serving (2 pancakes) with ¼ cup sliced strawberries and 1 to 2 tablespoons strawberry yogurt.

Betty Tip

Besides being a whole grain, whole wheat flour adds a nutty flavor and wholesome texture to these great-tasting pancakes. If you are new to whole grains, you can start by using ¾ cup whole wheat flour and ¾ cup all-purpose flour until you get used to the new flavor and texture.

1 Serving: Calories 260 (Calories from Fat 80); Total Fat 9g (Saturated Fat 1.5g; Trans Fat 0g); Cholesterol 95mg; Sodium 390mg; Total Carbohydrate 34g (Dietary Fiber 4g; Sugars 14g); Protein 9g
% Daily Value: Vitamin A 4%; Vitamin C 40%; Calcium 15%; Iron 8% **Exchanges:** 1½ Starch, 1 Other Carbohydrate, ½ Medium-Fat Meat, 1 Fat **Carbohydrate Choices:** 2

Oatmeal Pancakes
with Maple-Cranberry Syrup

PREP TIME: **25 MINUTES** • START TO FINISH: **25 MINUTES** • **6 SERVINGS** • WHOLE GRAIN SERVING: **½**

Syrup
½ cup maple-flavored syrup

¼ cup whole berry cranberry
    sauce

Pancakes
½ cup old-fashioned or
    quick-cooking oats

¼ cup all-purpose flour

¼ cup whole wheat flour

¾ cup buttermilk

¼ cup milk

1 tablespoon sugar

2 tablespoons canola oil

1 teaspoon baking powder

½ teaspoon baking soda

½ teaspoon salt

1 egg

1   In 1-quart saucepan, heat syrup ingredients over medium heat, stirring occasionally, until cranberry sauce is melted; keep warm.

2   Heat griddle to 375°F or heat 12-inch skillet over medium heat. Grease with canola oil if necessary (or spray with cooking spray before heating).

3   In medium bowl, beat all pancake ingredients with egg beater or wire whisk just until smooth. (For thinner pancakes, stir in additional 2 to 4 tablespoons milk.) For each pancake, pour slightly less than ¼ cup batter from cup or pitcher onto hot griddle. Cook pancakes until puffed and dry around edges. Turn; cook other sides until golden brown.

4   Top each serving (2 pancakes) with 2 tablespoons syrup.

Betty Tip
Old-fashioned oats are 100 percent whole grain; using them in baked goods adds a delightful, chewy texture and a burst of fiber.

1 Serving: Calories 250 (Calories from Fat 60); Total Fat 7g (Saturated Fat 1g; Trans Fat 0g); Cholesterol 40mg; Sodium 460mg; Total Carbohydrate 42g (Dietary Fiber 2g; Sugars 19g); Protein 5g **% Daily Value:** Vitamin A 0%; Vitamin C 0%; Calcium 10%; Iron 6% **Exchanges:** 1½ Starch, 1 Other Carbohydrate, 1½ Fat **Carbohydrate Choices:** 3

Upside-Down Date-Bran Muffins

PREP TIME: **20 MINUTES** • START TO FINISH: **40 MINUTES** • **12 MUFFINS** • WHOLE GRAIN SERVING: 1/2

Muffins

1 cup Fiber One® cereal

1 cup buttermilk

1/4 cup canola oil

1 teaspoon vanilla

1 egg

1 1/4 cups whole wheat flour

3/4 cup chopped dates

1/2 cup packed brown sugar

1 teaspoon baking soda

1/4 teaspoon salt

Topping

3 tablespoons packed brown sugar

2 tablespoons butter or margarine, melted

1 tablespoon light corn syrup

1 Heat oven to 400°F. Grease bottoms and sides of 12 regular-size muffin cups with shortening or cooking spray (do not use paper baking cups).

2 In blender or food processor, place cereal, buttermilk, oil, vanilla and egg. Cover; let stand 10 minutes. Meanwhile, in small bowl, stir all topping ingredients until well mixed. Place 1 teaspoon of the topping in bottom of each muffin cup.

3 Blend cereal mixture in blender on medium speed until smooth; set aside. In medium bowl, stir flour, dates, 1/2 cup brown sugar, the baking soda and salt until well mixed. Pour cereal mixture over flour mixture; stir just until moistened (batter will be thick). Divide batter evenly among muffin cups.

4 Bake 14 to 18 minutes or until toothpick inserted in center comes out clean. Immediately place cookie sheet upside down on muffin pan; turn cookie sheet and pan over to remove muffins. Serve warm if desired.

Betty Tip

You can make jumbo muffins, similar to the ones you see in the bakery. To make, just grease 6 jumbo muffin cups (3 1/2 × 2 1/4 inches) with shortening or cooking spray (do not use paper baking cups). Place 2 teaspoons of the topping in each cup before adding batter. Bake as directed.

1 Muffin: Calories 230 (Calories from Fat 70); Total Fat 8g (Saturated Fat 2g; Trans Fat 0g); Cholesterol 25mg; Sodium 220mg; Total Carbohydrate 36g (Dietary Fiber 5g; Sugars 21g); Protein 4g **% Daily Value:** Vitamin A 0%; Vitamin C 0%; Calcium 6%; Iron 10% **Exchanges:** 1 Starch, 1 1/2 Other Carbohydrate, 1 1/2 Fat **Carbohydrate Choices:** 2 1/2

Triple-Berry Oatmeal Muesli

PREP TIME: **25 MINUTES** • START TO FINISH: **40 MINUTES** • **6 SERVINGS** • WHOLE GRAIN SERVING: **2**

2¾ cups old-fashioned oats or rolled barley

½ cup sliced almonds

2 containers (6 oz each) banana crème or French vanilla low-fat yogurt

1½ cups milk

¼ cup ground flaxseed or flaxseed meal

½ cup fresh blueberries

½ cup fresh raspberries

½ cup sliced fresh strawberries

1   Heat oven to 350°F. On cookie sheet, spread oats and almonds. Bake 18 to 20 minutes, stirring occasionally, until light golden brown; cool 15 minutes.

2   In large bowl, mix yogurt and milk until well blended. Stir in oats, almonds and flaxseed. Top each serving with berries.

Betty Tip

This muesli is a combination of great-tasting, good-for-you foods, including whole-grain oats, flaxseed (the highest plant source of omega-3 fatty acids), yogurt and three kinds of berries.

1 Serving: Calories 320 (Calories from Fat 90); Total Fat 10g (Saturated Fat 2g; Trans Fat 0g); Cholesterol 5mg; Sodium 60mg; Total Carbohydrate 46g (Dietary Fiber 8g; Sugars 16g); Protein 13g **% Daily Value:** Vitamin A 8%; Vitamin C 10%; Calcium 20%; Iron 15% **Exchanges:** 2 Starch, 1 Other Carbohydrate, 1 High-Fat Meat **Carbohydrate Choices:** 3

Wild Rice Frittata

PREP TIME: **20 MINUTES** • START TO FINISH: **1 HOUR 35 MINUTES** • **6 SERVINGS** • WHOLE GRAIN SERVING: ½

½ cup uncooked wild rice

1¼ cups water

1 tablespoon butter or margarine

1 small green bell pepper, chopped (½ cup)

1 small red bell pepper, chopped (½ cup)

1 medium onion, chopped (½ cup)

6 eggs

¼ cup milk

1 cup shredded Swiss cheese (4 oz)

1 Cook wild rice in water as directed on package, or see page 16; drain if necessary.

2 In 10-inch nonstick skillet, melt butter over medium-high heat. Cook bell peppers and onion in butter 2 to 3 minutes, stirring frequently, until vegetables are crisp-tender.

3 In small bowl, mix eggs, milk, wild rice and ½ cup of the cheese; pour over vegetables. Reduce heat to medium-low. Cover; cook 15 to 20 minutes or until eggs are set. Remove from heat.

4 Sprinkle with remaining ½ cup cheese. Cover; let stand about 5 minutes or until cheese is melted. Cut into wedges. Serve immediately.

Betty Tip

Wild rice adds a chewy texture and nutty flavor to this fantastic frittata. If you prefer to use reduced-fat Swiss cheese, you can sometimes find it in the deli section of larger supermarkets.

1 Serving: Calories 240 (Calories from Fat 120); Total Fat 13g (Saturated Fat 6g; Trans Fat 0g); Cholesterol 235mg; Sodium 300mg; Total Carbohydrate 16g (Dietary Fiber 2g; Sugars 3g); Protein 14g
% Daily Value: Vitamin A 20%; Vitamin C 30%; Calcium 20%; Iron 6% **Exchanges:** 1 Starch, 1½ Medium-Fat Meat, 1 Fat **Carbohydrate Choices:** 1

Cranberry-Pecan Granola

PREP TIME: **30 MINUTES** • START TO FINISH: **30 MINUTES** • **8 SERVINGS** (¾ CUP EACH) • WHOLE GRAIN SERVING: **2**

3 cups old-fashioned oats

¼ cup chopped pecans

¼ cup frozen (thawed) orange juice concentrate

¼ cup real maple or maple-flavored syrup

½ teaspoon ground cinnamon

2 teaspoons canola oil

2 cups Wheat Chex® cereal

1⅓ cups sweetened dried cranberries (about 6 oz)

1   Heat oven to 325°F. In large bowl, mix oats and pecans.

2   In small bowl, mix juice concentrate, syrup, cinnamon and oil until well blended. Drizzle over oat mixture; toss well to coat evenly. Stir in cereal. Spread on 2 large cookie sheets or 2 (15 × 10 × 1-inch) pans.

3   Bake 20 to 25 minutes, stirring granola frequently and changing positions of cookie sheets once halfway through baking, until light golden brown. Stir half of cranberries into each half of granola.

Betty Tip

This fruity granola contains two whole grains: old-fashioned oats and whole-grain cereal. Eating one serving for breakfast gives you 2 whole-grain servings, putting you well on your way to 3 whole-grain servings daily.

1 Serving: Calories 320 (Calories from Fat 60); Total Fat 6g (Saturated Fat 0.5g; Trans Fat 0g); Cholesterol 0mg; Sodium 135mg; Total Carbohydrate 60g (Dietary Fiber 7g; Sugars 26g); Protein 7g **% Daily Value:** Vitamin A 4%; Vitamin C 10%; Calcium 6%; Iron 35% **Exchanges:** 2 Starch, 2 Other Carbohydrate, 1 Fat **Carbohydrate Choices:** 4

Baked Apple Oatmeal

PREP TIME: **15 MINUTES** • START TO FINISH: **1 HOUR** • **8 SERVINGS** • WHOLE GRAIN SERVING: **1½**

2⅔ cups old-fashioned oats

½ cup raisins

⅓ cup packed brown sugar

1 teaspoon ground cinnamon

¼ teaspoon salt

4 cups milk

2 medium apples or pears, chopped (2 cups)

½ cup chopped walnuts

Additional milk, if desired

1   Heat oven to 350°F. In 2-quart casserole, mix oats, raisins, brown sugar, cinnamon, salt, 4 cups milk and the apples.

2   Bake uncovered 40 to 45 minutes or until most liquid is absorbed. Sprinkle walnuts over top. Serve with additional milk.

Betty Tip

One serving of this oatmeal provides many nutrients: both soluble and insoluble fiber, iron, calcium, folic acid and that good-for-you fat, omega-3, from the walnuts! Keep leftovers on hand to reheat for another day.

1 Serving: Calories 300 (Calories from Fat 80); Total Fat 9g (Saturated Fat 2.5g; Trans Fat 0g); Cholesterol 10mg; Sodium 130mg; Total Carbohydrate 45g (Dietary Fiber 5g; Sugars 24g); Protein 10g **% Daily Value:** Vitamin A 4%; Vitamin C 0%; Calcium 20%; Iron 10% **Exchanges:** 1½ Starch, 1 Other Carbohydrate, ½ Low-Fat Milk, 1 Fat **Carbohydrate Choices:** 3

English Muffin Breakfast Pizzas

PREP TIME: **20 MINUTES** • START TO FINISH: **20 MINUTES** • **4 SERVINGS** • WHOLE GRAIN SERVING: **1**

4 eggs

¼ cup milk

Dash salt

Dash pepper

2 teaspoons canola oil

2 tablespoons chopped onion

2 tablespoons chopped red bell
pepper

2 tablespoons chopped cooked
ham

½ cup shredded reduced-fat
Cheddar cheese (2 oz)

2 100% whole wheat English
muffins, split, toasted

1 In small bowl, beat eggs, milk, salt and pepper with wire whisk or fork until well blended.

2 In 10-inch nonstick skillet, heat oil over medium heat. Cook onion, bell pepper and ham in oil 3 to 5 minutes, stirring occasionally, until vegetables are crisp-tender. Pour egg mixture into skillet. As eggs begin to set at bottom and side, gently lift cooked portions with spatula so that uncooked egg can flow to bottom. Cook 3 to 4 minutes or until eggs are thickened throughout but still moist. Stir in cheese.

3 Spoon egg mixture evenly over muffin halves.

Betty Tip

Let the kids have their own tasty pizzas for breakfast or dinner. This recipe is so easy, they'll love helping you make them, too. Another benefit? Kids eat better when they help prepare their meals.

1 Serving: Calories 210 (Calories from Fat 90); Total Fat 10g (Saturated Fat 3g; Trans Fat 0g); Cholesterol 220mg; Sodium 510mg; Total Carbohydrate 16g (Dietary Fiber 2g; Sugars 4g); Protein 14g **% Daily Value:** Vitamin A 10%; Vitamin C 8%; Calcium 25%; Iron 8% **Exchanges:** 1 Starch, 1½ Medium-Fat Meat, ½ Fat **Carbohydrate Choices:** 1

Fruit-Topped Breakfast Bagels

PREP TIME: **10 MINUTES** • START TO FINISH: **10 MINUTES** • **4 SERVINGS** • WHOLE GRAIN SERVING: **1**

⅓ cup diced banana

⅓ cup chopped fresh or canned (drained) peaches in juice

⅓ cup fresh raspberries

¼ cup orange or vanilla low-fat yogurt

2 100% whole wheat bagels, split

1 tablespoon prepared cinnamon-sugar

1 In small bowl, mix banana, peaches, raspberries and yogurt.

2 Toast bagels. Sprinkle cinnamon-sugar evenly over warm bagel halves. Top each bagel half with ¼ cup fruit mixture.

Betty Tip

You can use most any fresh fruits in place of the ones listed here—try chopped melon, apple or berries. Eating a whole grain at breakfast sets you up to easily eat three or more grain servings every day.

1 Serving: Calories 140 (Calories from Fat 5); Total Fat 0.5g (Saturated Fat 0g; Trans Fat 0g); Cholesterol 0mg; Sodium 100mg; Total Carbohydrate 29g (Dietary Fiber 3g; Sugars 11g); Protein 4g **% Daily Value:** Vitamin A 0%; Vitamin C 8%; Calcium 4%; Iron 6% **Exchanges:** 1 Starch, 1 Other Carbohydrate **Carbohydrate Choices:** 2

Apple-Cinnamon Breakfast Bread

PREP TIME: **20 MINUTES** • START TO FINISH: **2 HOURS 35 MINUTES** • **1 LOAF** (16 SLICES) • WHOLE GRAIN SERVING: ½

2 cups Total® cereal

1 cup apple juice or apple cider

½ teaspoon vanilla

1 cup whole wheat flour

1 cup all-purpose flour

¾ cup sugar

1½ teaspoons baking powder

1 teaspoon ground cinnamon

½ teaspoon baking soda

½ teaspoon salt

2 tablespoons canola oil

1 egg

1 medium unpeeled apple, chopped (1 cup)

1 Heat oven to 350°F. Grease bottom only of 9 × 5-inch loaf pan with shortening or cooking spray. Place cereal in resealable food-storage plastic bag or between sheets of waxed paper; crush with rolling pin. In large bowl, mix crushed cereal (about ¾ cup), apple juice and vanilla; let stand 10 minutes.

2 Stir remaining ingredients except apple into cereal mixture. Then, stir in apple. Pour into pan.

3 Bake 50 to 60 minutes or until toothpick inserted in center comes out clean. Cool 10 minutes. Loosen sides of loaf from pan; remove from pan to cooling rack. Cool completely before slicing, at least 1 hour.

Betty Tip

Use the cereal in your cupboard to add flavor and texture as well as whole-grain goodness to this terrific bread that's great any time of day.

1 Slice: Calories 140 (Calories from Fat 20); Total Fat 2.5g (Saturated Fat 0g; Trans Fat 0g); Cholesterol 15mg; Sodium 200mg; Total Carbohydrate 28g (Dietary Fiber 2g; Sugars 13g); Protein 3g **% Daily Value:** Vitamin A 2%; Vitamin C 8%; Calcium 20%; Iron 20% **Exchanges:** ½ Starch, 1½ Other Carbohydrate, ½ Fat **Carbohydrate Choices:** 2

Streusel-Topped Fruit Brunch Cake

PREP TIME: **15 MINUTES** • START TO FINISH: **1 HOUR** • **12 SERVINGS** • WHOLE GRAIN SERVING: ½

Cake

2 cups Wheat Chex® or
    Multi-Bran Chex® cereal

1½ cups orange juice

¼ cup canola oil

1 egg, slightly beaten

2 small bananas, thinly sliced

1 cup all-purpose flour

½ cup whole wheat flour

¾ cup granulated sugar

½ cup raisins, if desired

1 teaspoon baking soda

1 teaspoon ground cinnamon

½ teaspoon salt

Streusel Topping

½ cup Wheat Chex® or
    Multi-Bran Chex® cereal

½ cup chopped nuts, if desired

⅓ cup packed brown sugar

¼ cup all-purpose flour

2 tablespoons butter or
    margarine, softened

½ teaspoon ground cinnamon

1 Heat oven to 350°F. Grease bottom and sides of 9-inch square pan with shortening or cooking spray. In large bowl, mix 2 cups cereal and the orange juice; let stand about 2 minutes or until cereal is soft.

2 Stir oil, egg and bananas into cereal mixture. Stir in remaining cake ingredients. Spread in pan.

3 Bake 35 to 40 minutes or until top springs back when touched lightly in center. Meanwhile, place ½ cup cereal in resealable food-storage plastic bag or between sheets of waxed paper; coarsely crush with rolling pin. In small bowl, mix crushed cereal and remaining topping ingredients until crumbly.

4 When cake is done, set oven control to broil. Sprinkle topping evenly over warm cake. Broil with top about 5 inches from heat for 1 to 2 minutes or until bubbly (watch carefully to avoid burning).

Betty Tip

Fortified whole-grain cereals, like Chex® cereals, are a great source of vitamins and minerals, including iron—no cooking needed! This moist cake makes a terrific breakfast or brunch for family and friends.

1 Serving: Calories 280 (Calories from Fat 70); Total Fat 7g (Saturated Fat 1.5g; Trans Fat 0g); Cholesterol 25mg; Sodium 340mg; Total Carbohydrate 50g (Dietary Fiber 3g; Sugars 25g); Protein 4g **% Daily Value:** Vitamin A 6%; Vitamin C 15%; Calcium 4%; Iron 30% **Exchanges:** 1½ Starch, 2 Other Carbohydrate, 1 Fat **Carbohydrate Choices:** 3

Mixed-Berry Coffee Cake

PREP TIME: **15 MINUTES** • START TO FINISH: **1 HOUR** • **8 SERVINGS** • WHOLE GRAIN SERVING: **½**

¼ cup low-fat granola

½ cup buttermilk

⅓ cup packed brown sugar

2 tablespoons canola oil

1 teaspoon vanilla

1 egg

1 cup whole wheat flour

½ teaspoon baking soda

½ teaspoon ground cinnamon

⅛ teaspoon salt

1 cup mixed berries (such as blueberries, raspberries and blackberries)

1 Heat oven to 350°F. Spray 8- or 9-inch round pan with cooking spray. Place granola in resealable food-storage plastic bag or between sheets of waxed paper; slightly crush with rolling pin. Set aside.

2 In large bowl, stir buttermilk, brown sugar, oil, vanilla and egg together until smooth. Stir in flour, baking soda, cinnamon and salt just until moistened. Gently fold in half of the berries. Spoon into pan. Sprinkle with remaining berries and the granola.

3 Bake 28 to 33 minutes or until golden brown and top springs back when touched in center. Cool in pan on cooling rack 10 minutes. Serve warm.

Betty Tip

The low-fat granola and whole wheat flour in this tasty coffee cake give you two whole grains. The vanilla, cinnamon and nutmeg add flavor and help bring out the natural sweetness in baked goods so you don't need to add a lot of extra sugar.

1 Serving: Calories 160 (Calories from Fat 45); Total Fat 5g (Saturated Fat 0.5g; Trans Fat 0g); Cholesterol 30mg; Sodium 150mg; Total Carbohydrate 26g (Dietary Fiber 3g; Sugars 13g); Protein 4g **% Daily Value:** Vitamin A 2%; Vitamin C 0%; Calcium 4%; Iron 6% **Exchanges:** 1 Starch, ½ Other Carbohydrate, 1 Fat **Carbohydrate Choices:** 2

Sausage, Cheese and Tomato Strata

PREP TIME: **15 MINUTES** • START TO FINISH: **2 HOURS 55 MINUTES** • **12 SERVINGS** • WHOLE GRAIN SERVING: ½

1 lb bulk turkey sausage

8 slices 100% whole wheat bread, cut into 1-inch cubes (7 cups)

2 cups shredded Gruyère cheese (8 oz)

2 cups chopped plum (Roma) tomatoes (6 medium)

6 eggs

2 cups milk

2 teaspoons dried basil leaves

2 teaspoons Dijon mustard

1/2 teaspoon salt

1 In 10-inch skillet, cook sausage over medium-high heat 5 to 7 minutes, stirring occasionally, until no longer pink; drain.

2 Spray 13 × 9-inch (3-quart) glass baking dish with cooking spray. Spread bread in baking dish. Spread cooked sausage evenly over bread. Sprinkle evenly with 1½ cups of the cheese and the tomatoes.

3 In medium bowl, beat eggs, milk, basil, mustard and salt with fork or wire whisk; pour over tomatoes. Sprinkle with remaining ½ cup cheese. Cover tightly; refrigerate at least 2 hours but no longer than 24 hours.

4 Heat oven to 350°F. Uncover baking dish; bake 35 to 40 minutes or until knife inserted in center comes out clean.

Betty Tip

Sensational on many counts, this strata is a great way to get whole grains—it comes from the bread. It's a super do-ahead breakfast or dinner, and it's so delicious and pretty, folks or guests will ask for more!

1 Serving: Calories 280 (Calories from Fat 130); Total Fat 15g (Saturated Fat 6g; Trans Fat 0.5g); Cholesterol 165mg; Sodium 610mg; Total Carbohydrate 14g (Dietary Fiber 2g; Sugars 6g); Protein 22g **% Daily Value:** Vitamin A 15%; Vitamin C 4%; Calcium 30%; Iron 10% **Exchanges:** ½ Starch, ½ Other Carbohydrate, 3 Lean Meat, 1 Fat **Carbohydrate Choices:** 1

Spinach and Cheddar Quiche

PREP TIME: **20 MINUTES** • START TO FINISH: **1 HOUR 5 MINUTES** • **6 SERVINGS** • WHOLE GRAIN SERVING: ½

Crust

½ cup all-purpose flour

½ cup whole wheat flour

¼ teaspoon salt

¼ cup butter or margarine

3 to 4 tablespoons cold water

Filling

½ cup shredded reduced-fat sharp Cheddar cheese (2 oz)

1 tablespoon all-purpose flour

4 eggs, slightly beaten

1½ cups milk

½ teaspoon salt

1 cup firmly packed fresh spinach leaves, coarsely chopped

1 small red bell pepper, chopped (½ cup)

1 Heat oven to 375°F. In medium bowl, mix ½ cup all-purpose flour, the whole wheat flour and ¼ teaspoon salt. Cut in butter, using pastry blender (or pulling 2 table knives through ingredients in opposite directions), until mixture looks like small crumbs. Sprinkle with water, 1 tablespoon at a time, tossing with fork just until flour is moistened. Shape into ball; flatten slightly.

2 On floured surface, roll dough into 12-inch round. Fold dough into fourths; place in 9-inch glass pie plate. Unfold and ease into pie plate, pressing firmly against bottom and side; crimp edge. Trim overhanging edge of pastry 1 inch from rim of pie plate. Fold and roll pastry under, even with plate; flute.

3 In large bowl, mix cheese and 1 tablespoon flour. Stir in eggs, milk and ½ teaspoon salt until well blended. Stir in spinach and bell pepper. Pour into pie crust.

4 Bake 15 minutes. Cover edge of crust with strip of foil to keep crust from overbrowning. Bake 15 to 20 minutes longer or until knife inserted in center comes out clean. Let stand 10 minutes before serving.

Betty Tip

You may notice a "stamp" on food packages, telling you how many grams of whole grain is in the product. Use this to help you get to 48 grams of whole grain per day, the amount recommended by the USDA 2005 Dietary Guidelines.

1 Serving: Calories 250 (Calories from Fat 120); Total Fat 13g (Saturated Fat 7g; Trans Fat 0.5g); Cholesterol 170mg; Sodium 510mg; Total Carbohydrate 21g (Dietary Fiber 2g; Sugars 4g); Protein 11g **% Daily Value:** Vitamin A 30%; Vitamin C 20%; Calcium 15%; Iron 8% **Exchanges:** 1 Starch, ½ Other Carbohydrate, 1 Medium-Fat Meat, 1½ Fat **Carbohydrate Choices:** 1½

Berry-Banana Smoothie

PREP TIME: **10 MINUTES** • START TO FINISH: **10 MINUTES** • **2 SERVINGS** (ABOUT 1 CUP EACH) • WHOLE GRAIN SERVING: **½**

1 cup vanilla, plain, strawberry or raspberry low-fat yogurt

¾ cup Cheerios® cereal

2 tablespoons ground flaxseed or flaxseed meal

½ cup fresh strawberry halves, fresh raspberries or frozen whole strawberries

½ cup milk

1 to 2 tablespoons sugar

½ banana

1 In blender, place all ingredients. Cover; blend on high speed 10 seconds. Stop blender to scrape sides. Cover; blend about 20 seconds longer or until smooth.

2 Pour mixture into glasses. Serve immediately.

Betty Tip

Besides being refreshing, this smoothie is a great source of fiber, iron, calcium and vitamin C, and it contains ½ serving of whole grains.

1 Serving: Calories 290 (Calories from Fat 60); Total Fat 6g (Saturated Fat 2g; Trans Fat 0g); Cholesterol 10mg; Sodium 190mg; Total Carbohydrate 46g (Dietary Fiber 5g; Sugars 32g); Protein 11g **% Daily Value:** Vitamin A 8%; Vitamin C 45%; Calcium 35%; Iron 20% **Exchanges:** 1 Starch, ½ Fruit, 1 Other Carbohydrate, ½ Low-Fat Milk, ½ High-Fat Meat **Carbohydrate Choices:** 3

best breads

Five-Grain Quick Bread
Page 48

2

Two-Seed Checkerboard Dinner Rolls

PREP TIME: **40 MINUTES** • START TO FINISH: **3 HOURS 5 MINUTES** • **15 ROLLS** • WHOLE GRAIN SERVING: **½**

2 cups bread flour or
　　all-purpose flour
¼ cup honey
1 teaspoon salt
1 package regular active or
　　fast-acting dry yeast
1 cup very warm water
　　(120°F to 130°F)
3 tablespoons butter or
　　margarine, softened
1 egg
1½ to 2 cups whole wheat flour
1 egg white
1 teaspoon water
3 tablespoons sesame seed
2 tablespoons poppy seed

1　In large bowl, mix bread flour, honey, salt and yeast. Add warm water, butter and egg. Beat with electric mixer on low speed 1 minute, scraping bowl frequently. Beat on medium speed 1 minute, scraping bowl frequently. Stir in enough whole wheat flour to make dough easy to handle.

2　On lightly floured surface, knead dough about 5 minutes or until dough is smooth and springy. Grease large bowl with shortening or spray with cooking spray. Place dough in bowl, turning dough to grease all sides. Cover bowl loosely with plastic wrap; let rise in warm place about 1 hour or until it doubles in size. Dough is ready if indentation remains when touched.

3　Grease bottom and sides of 13 × 9-inch pan with shortening or spray with cooking spray. In small bowl, mix egg white and 1 teaspoon water with fork. Gently push fist into dough to deflate. Divide dough into 15 equal pieces. Shape each piece into a ball. Brush top of each ball with egg white mixture. Dip tops of 8 balls into sesame seed and tops of 7 balls into poppy seed. Arrange seed side up in checkerboard pattern in pan. Cover pan loosely with plastic wrap; let rise in warm place 45 to 60 minutes or until the balls double in size.

4　Heat oven to 375°F. Bake 17 to 21 minutes or until golden brown. Remove from pan to cooling rack. Serve warm or cooled.

Betty Tip

The sesame and poppy seeds and whole wheat flour give a crunchy, nutty flavor and texture that will make these super rolls a hit at your next dinner.

1 Roll: Calories 170 (Calories from Fat 40); Total Fat 4.5g (Saturated Fat 2g; Trans Fat 0g); Cholesterol 20mg; Sodium 180mg; Total Carbohydrate 28g (Dietary Fiber 2g; Sugars 5g); Protein 5g **% Daily Value:** Vitamin A 0%; Vitamin C 0%; Calcium 2%; Iron 10% **Exchanges:** 1½ Starch, ½ Other Carbohydrate, ½ Fat **Carbohydrate Choices:** 2

Five-Grain Quick Bread

PREP TIME: **15 MINUTES** • START TO FINISH: **50 MINUTES** • **1 LOAF** (12 SLICES) • WHOLE GRAIN SERVING: **2**

1 cup 5-grain rolled
    whole-grain cereal
    or old-fashioned oats

2 cups whole wheat flour

1 cup all-purpose flour

⅓ cup packed brown sugar

1 teaspoon baking soda

1 teaspoon cream of tartar

¾ teaspoon salt

¼ cup firm butter or margarine,
    cut into small pieces

½ cup golden raisins

1 egg

1½ cups buttermilk

1 Heat oven to 375°F. Grease cookie sheet with shortening or cooking spray. Reserve 1 tablespoon of the cereal.

2 In large bowl, mix remaining cereal, the flours, brown sugar, baking soda, cream of tartar and salt. Cut in butter, using pastry blender (or pulling 2 table knives through ingredients in opposite directions), until mixture looks like course crumbs. Stir in raisins.

3 In small bowl, beat egg and buttermilk with wire whisk until well blended. Reserve 1 tablespoon buttermilk mixture. Stir remaining buttermilk mixture into dry ingredients, stirring just until mixture is moistened. On floured surface, knead dough 5 or 6 times until dough is combined and holds together.

4 On cookie sheet, shape and press dough into 7-inch round. Cut large X, ¼ inch deep, into top of dough, using sharp knife. Brush top of dough with reserved buttermilk mixture; sprinkle with reserved cereal.

5 Bake 30 to 35 minutes or until top is golden brown and loaf sounds hollow when tapped. Cool slightly before serving.

Betty Tip

This old-fashioned soda bread is moist and flavorful, quick to make and a great choice to serve with soup or when entertaining. Whole wheat flour contains all parts of the grain, including the germ, so store it in the refrigerator to keep it fresh.

1 Slice: Calories 260 (Calories from Fat 50); Total Fat 6g (Saturated Fat 3g; Trans Fat 0g); Cholesterol 30mg; Sodium 320mg; Total Carbohydrate 43g (Dietary Fiber 4g; Sugars 11g); Protein 7g **% Daily Value:** Vitamin A 4%; Vitamin C 0%; Calcium 6%; Iron 10% **Exchanges:** 2 Starch, 1 Other Carbohydrate, 1 Fat **Carbohydrate Choices:** 3

Raisin Brown Bread

PREP TIME: **15 MINUTES** • START TO FINISH: **1 HOUR 15 MINUTES** • **32 SERVINGS** • WHOLE GRAIN SERVING: ½

1 cup all-purpose flour

1 cup whole wheat flour

1 cup whole-grain cornmeal

1 cup raisins

2 cups buttermilk

¾ cup molasses

2 teaspoons baking soda

1 teaspoon salt

1 Heat oven to 325°F. Grease 2-quart casserole dish with shortening or cooking spray.

2 In large bowl, beat all ingredients with electric mixer on low speed 30 seconds, scraping bowl constantly. Beat on medium speed 30 seconds, scraping bowl constantly. Pour batter into casserole.

3 Bake uncovered about 1 hour or until toothpick inserted in center comes out clean.

4 Immediately loosen sides of bread with metal spatula and unmold bread; cool on wire rack.

Steamed Brown Bread: Remove labels from four 4¼ × 3-inch cans (15- to 16-ounce vegetable cans). Grease cans or heatproof 7-inch tube mold with shortening or cooking spray. Make batter as directed. Fill cans about ⅔ full. Cover tightly with foil. Place cans on rack in Dutch oven or steamer; pour boiling water into pan to level of rack. Cover pan. Keep water boiling over low heat about 3 hours or until toothpick inserted in center comes out clean. (Add boiling water during steaming if necessary.)

Betty Tip

Created in Colonial times and called Boston Brown Bread, this authentic dark bread is made with cornmeal and molasses. Originally, it called for rye meal, which was available at the time. If you really like rye, use ½ cup of rye flour and ½ cup of whole wheat flour (in addition to the all-purpose flour).

1 Serving: Calories 90 (Calories from Fat 0); Total Fat 0.5g (Saturated Fat 0g; Trans Fat 0g); Cholesterol 0mg; Sodium 170mg; Total Carbohydrate 19g (Dietary Fiber 0g; Sugars 8g); Protein 2g **% Daily Value:** Vitamin A 0%; Vitamin C 0%; Calcium 4%; Iron 6% **Exchanges:** 1 Starch **Carbohydrate Choices:** 1

Honey—Whole Wheat Bread

PREP TIME: **20 MINUTES** • START TO FINISH: **3 HOURS 30 MINUTES** • **2 LOAVES** (16 SLICES EACH) • WHOLE GRAIN SERVING: **1**

2 packages regular active or fast-acting dry yeast

½ cup warm water (105°F to 115°F)

⅓ cup honey

¼ cup butter or margarine, softened

2 teaspoons salt

1¾ cups warm water (105°F to 115°F)

5 to 5¼ cups whole wheat flour

Additional butter or margarine, softened

Betty Tip

This super homemade bread gives you a wonderful wheaty flavor with fantastic volume and is 100% whole wheat. It also makes tasty toast the next day!

1 In large bowl, dissolve yeast in ½ cup warm water. Add honey, ¼ cup butter, the salt, 1¾ cups warm water and 4 cups of the whole wheat flour. Beat with electric mixer on low speed 1 minute, scraping bowl frequently. Beat on medium speed 1 minute, scraping bowl frequently. Stir in enough of the remaining 1 to 1¼ cups flour to make dough easy to handle.

2 On lightly floured surface, knead dough about 10 minutes or until smooth and springy. Grease large bowl with shortening or spray with cooking spray. Place dough in bowl, turning dough to grease all sides. Cover; let rise in warm place about 1 hour or until dough has doubled in size. Dough is ready if indentation remains when touched.

3 Grease bottoms and sides of 2 (9 × 5-inch or 8 × 4-inch) loaf pans with shortening or spray with cooking spray. Gently push fist into dough to deflate; divide in half. Flatten each half with hands or rolling pin into 18 × 9-inch rectangle. Fold crosswise into thirds, overlapping the 2 sides. Flatten or roll dough into 9-inch square. Roll dough up tightly, beginning at one of the open (unfolded) ends. Press with thumbs to seal after each turn. Pinch edge of dough into roll to seal. Pinch each end of roll to seal. Fold ends under loaf. Place seam side down in pan. Brush with additional butter; sprinkle with whole wheat flour or crushed oats if desired. Cover; let rise in warm place about 1 hour until dough has doubled in size.

4 Move oven rack to low position so that tops of pans will be in center of oven. Heat oven to 375°F. Bake 25 to 30 minutes or until loaves are deep golden brown and sound hollow when tapped. Remove from pans to cooling rack; cool.

1 Slice: Calories 100 (Calories from Fat 20); Total Fat 2g (Saturated Fat 1g; Trans Fat 0g); Cholesterol 0mg; Sodium 160mg; Total Carbohydrate 17g (Dietary Fiber 2g; Sugars 3g); Protein 3g **% Daily Value:** Vitamin A 0%; Vitamin C 0%; Calcium 0%; Iron 4% **Exchanges:** 1 Starch, ½ Fat **Carbohydrate Choices:** 1

Bread Machine Multigrain Loaf

PREP TIME: **10 MINUTES** • START TO FINISH: **3 HOURS 40 MINUTES** • **ONE 1½-POUND LOAF** (12 SLICES) •
WHOLE GRAIN SERVING: **1½**

1½ Pound (12 Slices)

1¼ cups water

2 tablespoons butter or
  margarine, softened

1⅓ cups bread flour

1⅓ cups whole wheat flour

1 cup uncooked 7-grain or
  multigrain hot cereal

3 tablespoons packed brown
  sugar

1¼ teaspoons salt

2½ teaspoons bread machine
  yeast *

2 Pound (16 Slices)

1½ cups water

2 tablespoons butter or
  margarine, softened

1½ cups bread flour

1½ cups whole wheat flour

1¼ cups uncooked 7-grain or
  multigrain hot cereal

¼ cup packed brown sugar

1½ teaspoons salt

2½ teaspoons bread machine
  yeast *

* The same amount of
yeast is needed for both the
1½-pound and 2-pound
recipes.

1 Make 1½-pound recipe with bread machines that use 3 cups flour, or make 2-pound recipe with bread machines that use 4 cups flour.

2 Measure carefully, placing all ingredients in bread machine pan in the order recommended by the manufacturer.

3 Select Basic/White cycle. Use Medium or Light crust color. Remove baked bread from pan; cool on cooking rack.

Betty Tip
You'll find 7-grain cereal in the hot cereal section of your supermarket or at a natural foods or co-op store.

1 Slice: Calories 180 (Calories from Fat 25); Total Fat 3g (Saturated Fat 1.5g; Trans Fat 0g); Cholesterol 5mg; Sodium 260mg; Total Carbohydrate 33g (Dietary Fiber 3g; Sugars 4g); Protein 5g **% Daily Value:** Vitamin A 0%; Vitamin C 0%; Calcium 0%; Iron 10% **Exchanges:** 2 Starch, ½ Fat **Carbohydrate Choices:** 2

Parmesan-Herb Breadsticks

PREP TIME: **15 MINUTES** • START TO FINISH: **1 HOUR** • **12 BREADSTICKS** • WHOLE GRAIN SERVING: **1**

Olive oil

Whole-grain cornmeal,
    if desired

12 frozen 100% whole wheat
    Texas bread dough rolls
    (from 48-oz package),
    thawed

2 tablespoons olive oil

3 or 4 long fresh rosemary
    sprigs

1 tablespoon grated Parmesan
    cheese

1   Brush 2 cookie sheets with olive oil; sprinkle with cornmeal. Roll each ball of dough into 9-inch rope. Place ropes about ½ inch apart on cookie sheets.

2   Brush 2 tablespoons olive oil over dough. Break 36 small clusters of rosemary leaves off rosemary sprigs. Using 3 clusters for each breadstick, insert stem end of each cluster ¼ inch deep into top of breadstick. Sprinkle cheese over dough. Cover loosely with plastic wrap; let rise in warm place about 30 minutes or until almost double in size.

3   Heat oven to 350°F. Bake 12 to 15 minutes or until light golden brown. Serve warm.

Betty Tip

These whole wheat and herb breadsticks make a sensational serve-with to any of the soups in Chapter 7, or a great whole-grain, any-time snack.

1 Breadstick: Calories 120 (Calories from Fat 40); Total Fat 4.5g (Saturated Fat 1g; Trans Fat 0g); Cholesterol 0mg; Sodium 200mg; Total Carbohydrate 17g (Dietary Fiber 2g; Sugars 4g); Protein 4g **% Daily Value:** Vitamin A 0%; Vitamin C 0%; Calcium 4%; Iron 6% **Exchanges:** 1 Starch, 1 Fat **Carbohydrate Choices:** 1

Blue Cornmeal Muffins

PREP TIME: **15 MINUTES** • START TO FINISH: **35 MINUTES** • **12 MUFFINS** • WHOLE GRAIN SERVING: **½**

1 cup whole-grain blue
    or yellow cornmeal
1 cup all-purpose flour
¼ cup sugar
1 cup buttermilk
¼ cup canola oil
1 teaspoon baking soda
1 teaspoon salt
1 egg

1   Heat oven to 400°F. Spray 12 regular-size muffin cups with cooking spray.

2   In large bowl, stir all ingredients with spoon just until ingredients are blended. Divide batter among muffin cups (about ¾ full).

3   Bake 18 to 21 minutes or until light golden brown. Immediately remove from pan. Serve warm.

Betty Tip

Corn was an important year-round staple for Native Americans, and it played a major role in the early days of American history. Today there are six varieties of corn available—white, yellow, red, blue, black and speckled. Choose whichever you like—the blue cornmeal makes a beautiful muffin.

1 Muffin: Calories 150 (Calories from Fat 50); Total Fat 6g (Saturated Fat 1g; Trans Fat 0g); Cholesterol 20mg; Sodium 320mg; Total Carbohydrate 22g (Dietary Fiber 0g; Sugars 5g); Protein 3g **% Daily Value:** Vitamin A 0%; Vitamin C 0%; Calcium 4%; Iron 6% **Exchanges:** 1 Starch, ½ Other Carbohydrate, 1 Fat **Carbohydrate Choices:** 1½

Wild Rice–Corn Muffins

PREP TIME: **10 MINUTES** • START TO FINISH: **1 HOUR 25 MINUTES** • **12 MUFFINS** • WHOLE GRAIN SERVING: ½

¼ cup uncooked wild rice

⅔ cup water

¾ cup milk

¼ cup canola oil

1 egg

½ cup all-purpose flour

½ cup whole wheat flour

½ cup sugar

½ cup whole-grain yellow cornmeal

2½ teaspoons baking powder

¼ teaspoon salt

½ cup chopped fresh or frozen cranberries

1   Cook wild rice in water as directed on package, or see page 16; drain if necessary. Cool 10 minutes.

2   Heat oven to 400°F. Spray 12 regular-size muffin cups with cooking spray, or line with paper baking cups.

3   In large bowl, mix milk, oil and egg. Stir in flours, sugar, cornmeal, baking powder and salt all at once just until flour is moistened. Fold in cooked wild rice and cranberries. Divide batter evenly among muffin cups.

4   Bake 20 to 25 minutes or until golden brown. Immediately remove from pan. Serve warm.

Betty Tip

Made with three whole grains (wild rice, cornmeal and whole wheat flour), this muffin looks and tastes wonderful and is terrific alongside a main-dish salad for lunch or dinner.

1 Muffin: Calories 160 (Calories from Fat 50); Total Fat 6g (Saturated Fat 0.5g; Trans Fat 0g); Cholesterol 20mg; Sodium 160mg; Total Carbohydrate 25g (Dietary Fiber 1g; Sugars 10g); Protein 3g **% Daily Value:** Vitamin A 0%; Vitamin C 0%; Calcium 8%; Iron 6% **Exchanges:** 1 Starch, ½ Other Carbohydrate, 1 Fat **Carbohydrate Choices:** 1½

Double-Chocolate Muffins

PREP TIME: **15 MINUTES** • START TO FINISH: **35 MINUTES** • **12 MUFFINS** • WHOLE GRAIN SERVING: **½**

1 cup Fiber One® cereal

1⅓ cups buttermilk

¼ cup canola oil

1 egg

¾ cup packed brown sugar

½ cup whole wheat flour

½ cup all-purpose flour

½ cup unsweetened baking cocoa

1 teaspoon baking soda

1 teaspoon vanilla

¼ teaspoon salt

⅓ cup miniature chocolate chips

1 Heat oven to 375°F. Place paper baking cup in each of 10 regular-size muffin cups. Place cereal in resealable food-storage plastic bag or between sheets of waxed paper; crush with rolling pin.

2 In medium bowl, stir crushed cereal and buttermilk; let stand 5 minutes. Stir in oil and egg. Stir in remaining ingredients except chocolate chips. Stir in chocolate chips. Divide batter evenly among muffin cups.

3 Bake 15 to 20 minutes or until toothpick inserted in center comes out clean. Immediately remove from pan. Serve warm.

Betty Tip

Not only are these fantastic muffins really yummy, but also they are packed with fiber. Fiber is the part of plant foods your body cannot digest, and it helps keep you regular. Getting fiber from a variety of food sources every day is an important part of good health.

1 Muffin: Calories 210 (Calories from Fat 70); Total Fat 7g (Saturated Fat 2g); Cholesterol 20mg; Sodium 360mg; Potassium 220mg; Total Carbohydrate 31g (Dietary Fiber 4g); Protein 4g
% Daily Value: Vitamin A 2%; Vitamin C 0%; Calcium 8%; Iron 10%; Vitamin D 2%; Folic Acid 8%
Exchanges: 1 Starch, 1½ Other Carbohydrate, 1½ Fat **Carbohydrate Choices:** 2

Oatmeal-Blueberry Muffins

PREP TIME: **15 MINUTES** • START TO FINISH: **40 MINUTES** • **12 MUFFINS** • WHOLE GRAIN SERVING: ½

1 cup buttermilk

1 cup old-fashioned oats

⅓ cup canola oil

½ cup packed brown sugar

1 egg

½ cup whole wheat flour

½ cup all-purpose flour

1 teaspoon baking soda

1 teaspoon ground cinnamon

¼ teaspoon salt

1 cup fresh or frozen (thawed and drained) blueberries

1   Heat oven to 400°F. Grease bottoms only of 12 regular-size muffin cups with shortening or cooking spray, or place paper baking cup in each muffin cup. In small bowl, pour buttermilk over oats.

2   In large bowl, mix oil, brown sugar and egg with spoon. Stir in flours, baking soda, cinnamon and salt just until flours are moistened. Stir in oat mixture; fold in blueberries. Divide batter evenly among muffin cups.

3   Bake 15 to 20 minutes or until golden brown. Cool 5 minutes before removing from pan. Serve warm.

Betty Tip

The combination of old-fashioned oats and whole wheat flour gives this hearty muffin a homespun look and taste. Why is it called whole wheat flour? Because it contains the whole grain, including all parts of the kernel: bran, the outer shell; endosperm, the inner part; and wheat germ, the embryo where many nutrients are stored.

1 Muffin: Calories 180 (Calories from Fat 70); Total Fat 8g (Saturated Fat 1g; Trans Fat 0g); Cholesterol 20mg; Sodium 180mg; Total Carbohydrate 24g (Dietary Fiber 2g; Sugars 11g); Protein 4g
% Daily Value: Vitamin A 0%; Vitamin C 0%; Calcium 4%; Iron 6% **Exchanges:** 1 Starch, ½ Other Carbohydrate, 1½ Fat **Carbohydrate Choices:** 1½

Cheesy Mexican Cornbread

PREP TIME: **10 MINUTES** • START TO FINISH: **40 MINUTES** • **12 SERVINGS** • WHOLE GRAIN SERVING: **1**

1½ cups whole-grain yellow cornmeal

½ cup all-purpose flour

1 cup shredded reduced-fat Monterey Jack or Cheddar cheese (4 oz)

¼ cup sugar

2 teaspoons baking powder

1 teaspoon salt

1 teaspoon chili powder

½ teaspoon baking soda

1 cup buttermilk

3 tablespoons canola oil

2 eggs

1 can (8.5 oz) cream-style corn

1 can (4.5 oz) chopped green chiles, well drained

1   Heat oven to 425°F. Grease 9-inch round cake pan, 8-inch square pan or 10-inch ovenproof skillet with shortening or cooking spray.

2   In medium bowl, mix all ingredients. Beat vigorously 30 seconds. Pour batter into pan.

3   Bake round or square pan 25 to 30 minutes, skillet about 20 minutes, or until golden brown. Serve warm.

Betty Tip

In this sweet and savory bread, the whole-grain corn adds a sweet flavor and is ideal for those looking for sweetness without mega fat and calories. This bread is a good choice to serve with chili, bean soup or any stew.

1 Serving: Calories 200 (Calories from Fat 70); Total Fat 7g (Saturated Fat 2g; Trans Fat 0g); Cholesterol 45mg; Sodium 640mg; Total Carbohydrate 27g (Dietary Fiber 2g; Sugars 7g); Protein 7g **% Daily Value:** Vitamin A 8%; Vitamin C 2%; Calcium 15%; Iron 8% **Exchanges:** 1 Starch, 1 Other Carbohydrate, ½ High-Fat Meat, ½ Fat **Carbohydrate Choices:** 2

Cornmeal-Berry Scones

PREP TIME: **15 MINUTES** • START TO FINISH: **40 MINUTES** • **12 SCONES** • WHOLE GRAIN SERVING: **1**

1 cup all-purpose flour

1 cup whole-grain yellow cornmeal

2 tablespoons granulated sugar

2 teaspoons baking powder

½ teaspoon baking soda

¼ teaspoon grated orange or lemon peel

¼ teaspoon salt

6 tablespoons firm butter, cut into cubes

½ cup vanilla soymilk

1 tablespoon orange juice

1½ cups fresh strawberries, coarsely chopped

1 tablespoon vanilla soymilk

1 to 2 tablespoons coarse sugar

1   Heat oven to 425°F. Spray cookie sheet with cooking spray, or line with cooking parchment paper.

2   In large bowl, mix flour, cornmeal, granulated sugar, baking powder, baking soda, grated orange peel and salt. Cut in butter, using pastry blender (or pulling 2 table knives through ingredients in opposite directions), just until mixture looks like coarse crumbs. Stir in ½ cup soymilk and the orange juice just until flour is moistened. Fold in strawberries.

3   Place dough on floured surface. Knead 6 to 8 times to form a ball. Divide in half; shape each half into 6 × ½-inch round on cookie sheet. Brush rounds with 1 tablespoon soymilk; sprinkle with 1 to 2 tablespoons coarse sugar. Cut each round into 6 wedges.

4   Bake 12 to 15 minutes or until tops are lightly browned. Cool 10 minutes. Separate wedges; serve warm.

Betty Tip

As tempting as it may be to eat these scones right away, they taste even better after cooling for at least 10 minutes. The extra cooling time allows the scones to become set, making them more tender.

1 Scone: Calories 160 (Calories from Fat 60); Total Fat 6g (Saturated Fat 3.5g; Trans Fat 0g); Cholesterol 15mg; Sodium 230mg; Total Carbohydrate 23g (Dietary Fiber 1g; Sugars 5g); Protein 3g **% Daily Value:** Vitamin A 4%; Vitamin C 10%; Calcium 6%; Iron 6%   **Exchanges:** 1 Starch, ½ Other Carbohydrate, 1 Fat   **Carbohydrate Choices:** 1½

Orange-Cranberry Scones

PREP TIME: **20 MINUTES** • START TO FINISH: **35 MINUTES** • **12 SCONES** • WHOLE GRAIN SERVING: **½**

Scones

2 cups Oatmeal Crisp® Raisin cereal

¾ cup all-purpose flour

¼ cup whole wheat flour

¼ cup packed brown sugar

2 teaspoons baking powder

1 teaspoon grated orange peel

¼ teaspoon salt

¼ cup firm butter or margarine

½ cup sweetened dried cranberries

1 egg, slightly beaten

¼ cup orange low-fat yogurt

Orange Glaze

½ cup powdered sugar

¼ teaspoon grated orange peel

2 to 3 teaspoons orange juice

1 Heat oven to 400°F. Place cereal in resealable food-storage plastic bag or between sheets of waxed paper; slightly crush with rolling pin.

2 In medium bowl, mix flours, brown sugar, baking powder, 1 teaspoon orange peel and the salt. Cut in butter, using pastry blender (or pulling 2 table knives through ingredients in opposite directions), until mixture looks like coarse crumbs. Stir in cereal, cranberries, egg and yogurt until soft dough forms.

3 On lightly floured surface, gently roll dough in flour to coat; shape into ball. Pat dough into 8-inch round with floured hands. Cut round into 12 wedges with sharp knife dipped in flour. On ungreased cookie sheet, place wedges about 1 inch apart.

4 Bake 7 to 9 minutes or until edges are light brown. Meanwhile, in small bowl, mix all glaze ingredients until smooth and thin enough to drizzle.

5 Immediately remove scones from cookie sheet to cooling rack. Cool 5 minutes; drizzle with glaze. Serve warm.

Betty Tip

These delicious scones have the goodness and chewy texture of whole-grain cereal and cranberries. To store scones, wait until the glaze has set, then store tightly covered.

1 Scone: Calories 180 (Calories from Fat 45); Total Fat 5g (Saturated Fat 2.5g; Trans Fat 0g); Cholesterol 30mg; Sodium 210mg; Total Carbohydrate 31g (Dietary Fiber 2g; Sugars 17g); Protein 3g **% Daily Value:** Vitamin A 2%; Vitamin C 0%; Calcium 6%; Iron 8% **Exchanges:** 1 Starch, 1 Other Carbohydrate, 1 Fat **Carbohydrate Choices:** 2

Hearty Three-Grain Biscuits

PREP TIME: **10 MINUTES** • START TO FINISH: **25 MINUTES** • **10 BISCUITS** • WHOLE GRAIN SERVING: **½**

¾ cup whole wheat flour

½ cup all-purpose flour

½ cup whole-grain cornmeal

3 teaspoons baking powder

¼ teaspoon salt

¼ cup shortening

½ cup old-fashioned or
    quick-cooking oats

About ¾ cup milk

1 Heat oven to 450°F. In large bowl, mix flours, cornmeal, baking powder and salt. Cut in shortening, using pastry blender (or pulling 2 table knives through ingredients in opposite directions), until mixture looks like fine crumbs. Stir in oats. Stir in just enough milk so dough leaves side of bowl and forms a ball.

2 On lightly floured surface, knead dough lightly 10 times. Roll or pat ½ inch thick. Cut with floured 2½-inch round cutter. On ungreased cookie sheet, place biscuits about 1 inch apart for crusty sides, touching for soft sides. Brush with milk and sprinkle with additional oats if desired.

3 Bake 10 to 12 minutes or until golden brown. Immediately remove from cookie sheet. Serve warm.

Betty Tip

These tasty biscuits contain three grains: cornmeal, whole wheat and oats. Combining grains add flavor, texture, variety and fun.

1 Biscuit: Calories 150 (Calories from Fat 50); Total Fat 6g (Saturated Fat 1.5g; Trans Fat 1g); Cholesterol 0mg; Sodium 210mg; Total Carbohydrate 21g (Dietary Fiber 2g; Sugars 1g); Protein 4g **% Daily Value:** Vitamin A 0%; Vitamin C 0%; Calcium 10%; Iron 6% **Exchanges:** 1 Starch, ½ Other Carbohydrate, 1 Fat **Carbohydrate Choices:** 1½

Best-Ever Oatmeal Brown Bread

PREP TIME: **10 MINUTES** • START TO FINISH: **3 HOURS 10 MINUTES** • **1 LOAF** (16 SLICES) • WHOLE GRAIN SERVING: ½

1½ cups whole wheat flour

1 cup all-purpose flour

⅔ cup packed dark brown sugar

½ cup old-fashioned oats

⅓ cup ground flaxseed or flaxseed meal

1 teaspoon baking soda

1 teaspoon salt

1⅔ cups buttermilk

1   Heat oven to 350°F. Spray 8 × 4-inch loaf pan with cooking spray.

2   In large bowl, mix flours, brown sugar, oats, the flaxseed, baking soda and salt. Stir in buttermilk just until mixed. Pour batter into pan. Sprinkle with 1 tablespoon oats.

3   Bake 45 to 55 minutes or until toothpick inserted in center comes out clean. Cool in pan on cooling rack 5 minutes. Remove from pan to cooling rack. Cool completely, about 2 hours, before slicing.

Betty Tip

Oats, whole wheat flour and flaxseed is a winning combination for a deliciously moist bread that's even better toasted the next day. The flaxseed in this recipe replaces eggs and much of the oil that is used in other quick breads.

1 Slice: Calories 140 (Calories from Fat 15); Total Fat 2g (Saturated Fat 0g; Trans Fat 0g); Cholesterol 0mg; Sodium 250mg; Total Carbohydrate 27g (Dietary Fiber 3g; Sugars 10g); Protein 4g   **% Daily Value:** Vitamin A 0%; Vitamin C 0%; Calcium 6%; Iron 8% **Exchanges:** 1 Starch, 1 Other Carbohydrate   **Carbohydrate Choices:** 2

S'more Swirl Bread

PREP TIME: **20 MINUTES** • START TO FINISH: **2 HOURS 40 MINUTES** • **1 LOAF** (16 SLICES) • WHOLE GRAIN SERVING: ½

Filling

¼ cup graham cracker crumbs

2 teaspoons sugar

¾ cup miniature marshmallows

1½ bars (1.55 oz each) milk chocolate candy, finely chopped

Bread

2 cups whole wheat flour

1 cup all-purpose flour

⅓ cup sugar

1 teaspoon salt

1 package regular active or fast-acting dry yeast

1¼ cups very warm milk (120°F to 130°F)

2 tablespoons canola oil

1 egg

2 teaspoons butter or margarine, melted

1   Grease bottom and sides of 9 × 5-inch or 8 × 4-inch loaf pan with shortening or cooking spray.

2   In small bowl, mix graham cracker crumbs and 2 teaspoons sugar. Reserve 2 teaspoons mixture for topping baked bread.

3   In large bowl, mix flours, sugar, the salt and yeast. Add warm milk, oil and egg; stir until flour is completely moistened and stiff batter forms. Spoon half of batter into pan, spreading completely to sides of pan.

4   In the following order, sprinkle batter with marshmallows, graham cracker mixture and chocolate, keeping at least a ½-inch border of uncovered batter on all sides. Spoon remaining batter as evenly as possible over filling; carefully and gently spread batter to sides of pan. Lightly spray sheet of plastic wrap with cooking spray; place sprayed side down loosely over pan. Let rise in warm place 1 hour to 1 hour 10 minutes or until dough has doubled in size.

5   Heat oven to 350°F. Bake 35 to 40 minutes or until top of loaf is deep golden brown and loaf sounds hollow when tapped. Immediately remove from pan to cooling rack. Brush top with melted butter; sprinkle with reserved 2 teaspoons graham cracker mixture. Cool 30 minutes.

Betty Tip

As unbelievably tasty as it is easy, this bread proves that you can have great flavor and get your whole grains at the same time. And yes, folks will clamor for s'more!

1 Slice: Calories 170 (Calories from Fat 40); Total Fat 4.5g (Saturated Fat 1.5g; Trans Fat 0g); Cholesterol 15mg; Sodium 180mg; Total Carbohydrate 28g (Dietary Fiber 2g; Sugars 10g); Protein 4g **% Daily Value:** Vitamin A 0%; Vitamin C 0%; Calcium 4%; Iron 6% **Exchanges:** ½ Starch, 1½ Other Carbohydrate, 1 Fat **Carbohydrate Choices:** 2

Three-Seed Flatbread

PREP TIME: **10 MINUTES** • START TO FINISH: **1 HOUR 15 MINUTES** • **12 SERVINGS** • WHOLE GRAIN SERVING: ½

6 frozen unbaked 100% whole wheat Texas bread dough rolls (from 48-oz package)

2 teaspoons olive oil

3 cloves garlic, finely chopped

1 teaspoon ground flaxseed or flaxseed meal

½ teaspoon black sesame seed or poppy seed

½ teaspoon white sesame seed

½ teaspoon salt

¼ teaspoon dried basil leaves

2 tablespoons shredded Parmesan cheese

1   On microwavable plate, place frozen rolls. Cover with microwavable plastic wrap; microwave on High 25 seconds. Turn rolls over; rotate plate ½ turn. Microwave on High 25 seconds longer to thaw.

2   Spray 13 × 9-inch pan with cooking spray. On lightly floured surface, knead roll dough together. Pat dough in bottom of pan; brush with oil. Sprinkle with remaining ingredients.

3   Cover; let rise in warm place about 40 minutes or until slightly puffy.

4   Heat oven to 350°F. Bake 20 to 22 minutes or until golden brown. Cut into 12 squares.

Betty Tip

The seeds add interest and great taste to this wonderful flatbread. Eating more seeds, though they're not whole grain, is also a good change for anyone's health. And a simple change like replacing butter with olive oil can help reduce the amount of saturated fat you eat.

1 Serving: Calories 70 (Calories from Fat 20); Total Fat 2g (Saturated Fat 0.5g; Trans Fat 0g); Cholesterol 0mg; Sodium 230mg; Total Carbohydrate 10g (Dietary Fiber 2g; Sugars 2g); Protein 3g **% Daily Value:** Vitamin A 0%; Vitamin C 0%; Calcium 4%; Iron 4% **Exchanges:** ½ Starch, ½ Fat **Carbohydrate Choices:** ½

Golden Harvest Bread

PREP TIME: **15 MINUTES** • START TO FINISH: **2 HOURS 35 MINUTES** • **1 LOAF** (16 SLICES) • WHOLE GRAIN SERVING: ½

1 can (8 oz) crushed pineapple
    in juice, undrained

2 tablespoons canola oil

1 egg

1¼ cups whole wheat flour

¾ cup packed brown sugar

½ cup raisins

1 teaspoon baking powder

½ teaspoon baking soda

½ teaspoon salt

½ teaspoon ground cinnamon

1 cup shredded carrots
    (1½ medium)

1 cup chopped walnuts

1 Heat oven to 350°F. Grease bottom and sides of 8 × 4-inch loaf pan with shortening or cooking spray.

2 In medium bowl, mix pineapple (with juice), oil and egg. Stir in remaining ingredients until blended. Spread batter in pan.

3 Bake 50 to 55 minutes or until toothpick inserted in center comes out clean. Cool 10 minutes. Remove from pan to cooling rack. Cool completely, about 1 hour, before slicing.

Betty Tip

This packed-with-yummy-ingredients bread is as beautiful as it is tasty and it makes a great snack or quick breakfast on your way out the door.

1 Slice: Calories 170 (Calories from Fat 60); Total Fat 7g (Saturated Fat 0.5g; Trans Fat 0g); Cholesterol 15mg; Sodium 160mg; Total Carbohydrate 24g (Dietary Fiber 2g; Sugars 15g); Protein 3g
% Daily Value: Vitamin A 15%; Vitamin C 0%; Calcium 4%; Iron 6% **Exchanges:** ½ Starch, 1 Other Carbohydrate, 1½ Fat **Carbohydrate Choices:** 1½

Fruit and Nut Bread
with Browned Butter Glaze

PREP TIME: **30 MINUTES** • START TO FINISH: **2 HOURS 55 MINUTES** • **1 LOAF** (16 SLICES) • WHOLE GRAIN SERVING: **½**

Bread

2¼ cups Multi-Bran Chex® cereal

1 cup all-purpose flour

1 cup whole wheat flour

2 teaspoons baking powder

1 teaspoon pumpkin pie spice

½ teaspoon salt

1 egg

1⅓ cups milk

¼ cup canola oil

⅓ cup dark molasses

½ cup chopped walnuts

¾ cup diced dried fruit and raisin mixture

Glaze

1 tablespoon butter (do not use margarine)

½ cup powdered sugar

1 teaspoon vanilla

2 teaspoons water

1   Heat oven to 375°F. Spray 8 × 4-inch loaf pan with cooking spray; dust with flour. Place cereal in resealable food-storage plastic bag or between sheets of waxed paper; coarsely crush with rolling pin.

2   In large bowl, mix crushed cereal, flours, baking powder, pumpkin pie spice and salt. Stir in egg, milk, oil and molasses just until well combined. Stir in walnuts and dried fruit. Pour into pan.

3   Bake 45 to 55 minutes or until toothpick inserted in center comes out clean. Cool in pan 30 minutes. Remove from pan to cooling rack. Cool completely, about 1 hour.

4   In 1-quart saucepan, heat butter over medium-low heat, stirring occasionally, until golden brown; remove from heat. Beat in remaining glaze ingredients with wire whisk until smooth; drizzle over loaf.

Betty Tip

Don't tell the kids! This fabulous bread with a luscious glaze is really good for them—it's got fiber, vitamins and minerals from the cereal and dried fruit.

1 Slice: Calories 220 (Calories from Fat 70); Total Fat 8g (Saturated Fat 1.5g; Trans Fat 0g); Cholesterol 15mg; Sodium 210mg; Total Carbohydrate 33g (Dietary Fiber 3g; Sugars 13g); Protein 4g **% Daily Value:** Vitamin A 4%; Vitamin C 0%; Calcium 10%; Iron 20% **Exchanges:** 1 Starch, 1 Other Carbohydrate, 1½ Fat **Carbohydrate Choices:** 2

Savory-Sweet Potato Pan Bread

PREP TIME: **15 MINUTES** • START TO FINISH: **40 MINUTES** • **8 SERVINGS** • WHOLE GRAIN SERVING: **½**

1½ cups uncooked shredded
   dark-orange sweet potato
   (about ½ potato)

½ cup sugar

¼ cup canola oil

2 eggs

¾ cup all-purpose flour

¾ cup whole wheat flour

2 teaspoons dried, minced
   onion

1 teaspoon dried rosemary
   leaves, crumbled

1 teaspoon baking soda

½ teaspoon salt

¼ teaspoon baking powder

2 teaspoons sesame seed

1   Heat oven to 350°F. Grease bottom only of 9-inch round cake pan with shortening or cooking spray.

2   In large bowl, mix sweet potato, sugar, oil and eggs. Stir in remaining ingredients except sesame seed. Spread batter in pan. Sprinkle sesame seed over batter.

3   Bake 20 to 25 minutes or until golden brown. Serve warm.

Betty Tip

Sweet potatoes add sweetness, extra flavor and color to this yummy savory bread. It's an excellent choice to serve with dinner, or eat as a snack. Keep leftovers tightly covered.

1 Serving: Calories 240 (Calories from Fat 80); Total Fat 9g (Saturated Fat 1g; Trans Fat 0g); Cholesterol 55mg; Sodium 340mg; Total Carbohydrate 34g (Dietary Fiber 3g; Sugars 15g); Protein 5g **% Daily Value:** Vitamin A 80%; Vitamin C 4%; Calcium 4%; Iron 8% **Exchanges:** 1 Starch, 1½ Other Carbohydrate, 1½ Fat **Carbohydrate Choices:** 2

grains on the go

Apricot-Almond Energy Bars
Page 76

3

On-the-Go Apple Breakfast Bars

PREP TIME: **30 MINUTES** • START TO FINISH: **2 HOURS 30 MINUTES** • **12 BARS** • WHOLE GRAIN SERVING: **½**

1½ cups dried apples, finely chopped

½ cup chopped pecans

3 cups Total® Raisin Bran cereal

⅓ cup honey

¼ cup golden raisins

1 tablespoon packed brown sugar

⅓ cup chunky or creamy peanut butter

¼ cup apple butter

½ teaspoon ground cinnamon

½ cup old-fashioned or quick-cooking oats

¼ cup roasted sunflower nuts

1   Line bottom and sides of 8-inch square pan with foil; spray foil with cooking spray. Sprinkle ½ cup of the apples and ¼ cup of the pecans over bottom of pan. Place cereal in resealable food-storage plastic bag or between sheets of waxed paper; coarsely crush with rolling pin. Set aside.

2   In 4-quart Dutch oven, heat ½ cup of the apples, the honey, raisins and brown sugar to boiling over medium-high heat, stirring occasionally. Reduce heat to medium. Cook uncovered about 1 minute, stirring constantly, until hot and bubbly; remove from heat.

3   Stir peanut butter into cooked mixture until melted. Stir in apple butter and cinnamon. Stir in oats and sunflower nuts until well mixed. Stir in crushed cereal.

4   Press mixture very firmly (or bars will crumble) and evenly onto apples and pecans in pan. Sprinkle with remaining ½ cup apples and ¼ cup pecans; press lightly into bars. Refrigerate about 2 hours or until set. For bars, cut into 4 rows by 3 rows. Store covered in refrigerator.

Betty Tip

The beauty of this whole-grain breakfast bar is that it can be made ahead and stored in the refrigerator. Its hearty flavor and texture make it ideal for days when "on the go" is a must.

1 Bar: Calories 250 (Calories from Fat 80); Total Fat 9g (Saturated Fat 1g; Trans Fat 0g); Cholesterol 0mg; Sodium 125mg; Total Carbohydrate 37g (Dietary Fiber 4g; Sugars 25g); Protein 4g **% Daily Value:** Vitamin A 2%; Vitamin C 0%; Calcium 25%; Iron 30% **Exchanges:** 1 Starch, 1½ Other Carbohydrate, 1½ Fat **Carbohydrate Choices:** 2½

Take-Along Oatmeal Bars

PREP TIME: **15 MINUTES** • START TO FINISH: **45 MINUTES** • **16 BARS** • WHOLE GRAIN SERVING: ½

¼ cup sugar

¼ cup butter or margarine

⅓ cup honey

½ teaspoon ground cinnamon

1 cup diced dried fruit and raisin mixture

2 cups Wheaties® cereal

1 cup old-fashioned or quick-cooking oats

½ cup sliced almonds

1   Grease bottom and sides of 9-inch square pan with small amount of butter.

2   In 3-quart saucepan, heat sugar, butter, honey and cinnamon to boiling over medium heat, stirring constantly. Boil 1 minute, stirring constantly; remove from heat. Stir in dried fruit. Stir in remaining ingredients.

3   Press mixture in pan with back of wooden spoon. Cool completely, about 30 minutes. For bars, cut into 4 rows by 4 rows. Store loosely covered at room temperature.

Betty Tip

These breakfast super-snacks contain both ready-to-eat cereal and oats, two great whole grains that are terrific together. Pack a couple bars in your backpack, lunch box or briefcase for a morning—or any time of day—energy boost.

1 Bar: Calories 140 (Calories from Fat 45); Total Fat 5g (Saturated Fat 2g; Trans Fat 0g); Cholesterol 10mg; Sodium 55mg; Total Carbohydrate 22g (Dietary Fiber 2g; Sugars 14g); Protein 2g
% Daily Value: Vitamin A 6%; Vitamin C 0%; Calcium 0%; Iron 10% **Exchanges:** ½ Starch, 1 Other Carbohydrate, 1 Fat **Carbohydrate Choices:** 1½

Chewy Peanut Bars

PREP TIME: **20 MINUTES** • START TO FINISH: **50 MINUTES** • **16 BARS** • WHOLE GRAIN SERVING: ½

4 cups Wheaties® cereal

⅓ cup lightly salted dry-roasted peanuts, coarsely chopped

½ cup light corn syrup

⅓ cup packed brown sugar

¼ cup peanut butter

3 tablespoons semisweet chocolate chips

1 Spray 9-inch square pan with cooking spray. In large bowl, mix cereal and peanuts.

2 In 2-quart saucepan, heat corn syrup, brown sugar and peanut butter to boiling over medium heat, stirring constantly. Boil and stir 1 minute. Pour over cereal mixture, stirring to coat entire mixture. Press in pan.

3 In small microwavable bowl, microwave chocolate chips uncovered on High 30 seconds; stir. Continue microwaving 10 seconds at a time, stirring after each microwave time, until smooth. Drizzle chocolate over bars. Refrigerate about 30 minutes or until chocolate has hardened. For bars, cut into 4 rows by 4 rows.

Betty Tip

These terrific-tasting bars go together in a hurry. If the cereal mixture is a bit sticky when you press it in the pan, dampen your hands first and use them to press the mixture.

1 Bar: Calories 140 (Calories from Fat 40); Total Fat 4.5g (Saturated Fat 1g; Trans Fat 0g); Cholesterol 0mg; Sodium 110mg; Total Carbohydrate 23g (Dietary Fiber 2g; Sugars 11g); Protein 3g **% Daily Value:** Vitamin A 4%; Vitamin C 0%; Calcium 0%; Iron 15% **Exchanges:** ½ Starch, 1 Other Carbohydrate, 1 Fat **Carbohydrate Choices:** 1½

Apricot-Almond Energy Bars

PREP TIME: **25 MINUTES** • START TO FINISH: **55 MINUTES** • **16 BARS** • WHOLE GRAIN SERVING: ½

3 cups Oatmeal Crisp® Raisin cereal

⅔ cup finely diced dried apricots

½ cup slivered almonds, toasted*

1 tablespoon butter or margarine

⅔ cup light corn syrup

¼ cup packed brown sugar

½ teaspoon ground cinnamon

* To toast nuts, bake uncovered in ungreased shallow pan in 350°F oven 6 to 10 minutes, stirring occasionally, until light brown. Or cook in ungreased heavy skillet over medium heat 5 to 7 minutes, stirring frequently until nuts begin to brown, then stirring constantly until nuts are light brown.

1   Line bottom and sides of 8-inch square pan with foil. Spray foil with cooking spray. In large bowl, mix cereal, apricots and almonds; set aside.

2   In 4-quart Dutch oven, heat butter, corn syrup, brown sugar and cinnamon over medium-high heat, stirring constantly, until sugar is dissolved and mixture comes to a boil. Boil 2 minutes, stirring constantly, until slightly thickened. Remove from heat. Stir in cereal mixture until coated.

3   Spread cereal mixture in pan. Using sheet of waxed paper, press mixture firmly in pan. Cool 30 minutes.

4   For bars, cut into 4 rows by 4 rows. Store loosely covered at room temperature up to 1 week.

Betty Tip

Lining the pan with nonstick foil works well for these glossy, great-tasting energy bars. For a quick snack, wrap a couple of bars individually in nonstick foil, and they'll be ready to go when you are.

1 Bar: Calories 140 (Calories from Fat 25); Total Fat 3g (Saturated Fat 0.5g; Trans Fat 0g); Cholesterol 0mg; Sodium 70mg; Total Carbohydrate 28g (Dietary Fiber 2g; Sugars 15g); Protein 2g **% Daily Value:** Vitamin A 4%; Vitamin C 0%; Calcium 0%; Iron 6% **Exchanges:** ½ Starch, 1½ Other Carbohydrate, ½ Fat **Carbohydrate Choices:** 2

Popcorn and Peanut Bars

PREP TIME: **15 MINUTES** • START TO FINISH: **45 MINUTES** • **9 BARS** • WHOLE GRAIN SERVING: ½

1¼ cups Wheaties® cereal

½ cup dry-roasted peanuts, chopped

¼ cup raisins

4 cups popped popcorn

½ cup pretzel sticks, broken

½ cup peanut butter chips

¼ cup honey

2 tablespoons chocolate chips

¼ teaspoon canola oil

1   Line bottom and sides of 9-inch square pan with foil. Spray foil with cooking spray.

2   In large bowl, mix cereal, peanuts, raisins, popcorn and pretzels.

3   In small microwavable bowl, microwave peanut butter chips and honey uncovered on High 1 to 2 minutes, stirring every 30 seconds, until smooth.

4   Pour peanut butter–honey mixture over cereal mixture. Stir to coat evenly. Spoon into pan. Using buttered fingers, press firmly so that mixture is even.

5   In small microwavable bowl, microwave chocolate chips and oil uncovered on High 30 to 60 seconds; stir until smooth. Drizzle chocolate over bars.

6   Refrigerate about 30 minutes or until firm. Remove mixture from pan; for bars, cut into 3 rows by 3 rows. Store covered in refrigerator up to 1 week.

Betty Tip

The honey adds a bit of sweetness to this salty-sweet whole-grain bar. Honey will slide easily out of the measuring cup if you first spray the cup with cooking spray. To save time, spray the cup at the same time you spray the foil in the pan.

1 Bar: Calories 170 (Calories from Fat 70); Total Fat 8g (Saturated Fat 1.5g; Trans Fat 0g); Cholesterol 0mg; Sodium 130mg; Total Carbohydrate 21g (Dietary Fiber 2g; Sugars 13g); Protein 4g **% Daily Value:** Vitamin A 0%; Vitamin C 0%; Calcium 0%; Iron 10%   **Exchanges:** ½ Starch, 1 Other Carbohydrate, 1½ Fat   **Carbohydrate Choices:** 1½

Trail Mix Bars

PREP TIME: **15 MINUTES** • START TO FINISH: **1 HOUR** • **20 BARS** • WHOLE GRAIN SERVING: ½

¼ cup butter or margarine

1 cup graham cracker crumbs

2 tablespoons sugar

1 cup miniature marshmallows

3 cups Wheat Chex® cereal

1½ cups thin pretzel sticks

¼ cup semisweet chocolate chips

¼ cup candy-coated chocolate candies

1 can (14 oz) fat-free sweetened condensed milk

1   Heat oven to 350°F. Place butter in 13 × 9-inch pan; place in oven 2 to 4 minutes or until melted. Sprinkle graham cracker crumbs and sugar over butter; mix well. Press mixture evenly in pan.

2   Layer marshmallows, cereal, pretzels, chocolate chips and candies over mixture in pan. Pour milk evenly over top.

3   Bake 25 minutes. Cool 5 minutes. Run knife along edge of pan to loosen. For bars, cut into 5 rows by 4 rows. Cool at least 15 minutes.

Betty Tip

These tasty cereal bars will remind you of the popular seven-layer bars, only these are made with whole-grain cereal.

1 Bar: Calories 220 (Calories from Fat 50); Total Fat 5g (Saturated Fat 3g; Trans Fat 0g); Cholesterol 10mg; Sodium 250mg; Total Carbohydrate 40g (Dietary Fiber 2g; Sugars 26g); Protein 4g
% Daily Value: Vitamin A 4%; Vitamin C 0%; Calcium 10%; Iron 20% **Exchanges:** 1 Starch, 1½ Other Carbohydrate, 1 Fat **Carbohydrate Choices:** 2½

Vanilla Cereal Chunks

PREP TIME: **15 MINUTES** • START TO FINISH: **30 MINUTES** • **16 SERVINGS** (½ CUP EACH) • WHOLE GRAIN SERVING: ½

½ cup semisweet chocolate chips

1 cup Corn Chex® cereal

1 cup Rice Chex® cereal

3 cups Wheat Chex® cereal

1 cup lightly salted dry-roasted peanuts

1 cup small pretzel twists

1 cup miniature marshmallows

10 oz (half of 20-oz package) vanilla-flavored candy coating (almond bark), chopped

1 Place chocolate chips in freezer to chill. In large bowl, mix cereals, peanuts, pretzels and marshmallows; set aside.

2 In large microwavable bowl, microwave candy coating uncovered on High 1 minute 30 seconds. Stir, breaking up large chunks. Microwave about 30 seconds longer or until coating can be stirred smooth.

3 Gently and quickly stir cereal mixture into coating with rubber spatula, stirring gently until evenly coated. Stir in chilled chocolate chips. Spread on waxed paper. Cool about 15 minutes. Break into chunks. Store in airtight container in refrigerator.

Betty Tip

Chilling the chocolate chips keeps them from melting completely when you stir them into the warm mixture. Store this snack in an airtight bag, or portion it into individual bags for a quick pick-me-up when you need it.

1 Serving: Calories 230 (Calories from Fat 90); Total Fat 10g (Saturated Fat 4.5g; Trans Fat 0g); Cholesterol 0mg; Sodium 210mg; Total Carbohydrate 32g (Dietary Fiber 2g; Sugars 17g); Protein 4g
% Daily Value: Vitamin A 4%; Vitamin C 0%; Calcium 8%; Iron 30% **Exchanges:** 1 Starch, 1 Other Carbohydrate, 2 Fat **Carbohydrate Choices:** 2

Creamy Apple-Cinnamon Quesadilla

PREP TIME: **20 MINUTES** • START TO FINISH: **20 MINUTES** • **4 SERVINGS** (2 WEDGES EACH) • WHOLE GRAIN SERVING: ½

1 tablespoon granulated sugar

¼ teaspoon ground cinnamon

¼ cup reduced-fat cream cheese spread (from 8-oz container)

1 tablespoon packed brown sugar

¼ teaspoon ground cinnamon

2 whole wheat tortillas (8 inch)

½ small apple, cut into ¼-inch slices (½ cup)

Cooking spray

1 In small bowl, mix granulated sugar and ¼ teaspoon cinnamon; set aside. In another small bowl, mix cream cheese, brown sugar and ¼ teaspoon cinnamon with spoon.

2 Spread cream cheese mixture over tortillas. Place apple slices on cream cheese mixture on 1 tortilla. Top with remaining tortilla, cheese side down. Spray both sides of quesadilla with cooking spray; sprinkle with cinnamon-sugar mixture.

3 Heat 10-inch nonstick skillet over medium heat. Cook quesadilla in skillet 2 to 3 minutes or until bottom is brown and crisp; turn quesadilla. Cook 2 to 3 minutes longer or until bottom is brown and crisp.

4 Remove from skillet to cutting board; let stand 2 to 3 minutes. Cut into 8 wedges.

Betty Tip

The whole wheat tortillas are the stars in this kid-friendly snack, which is so easy to prepare; the kids can make their own. If your family is not used to whole wheat tortillas, ask them to try something new—they may just like (or love) it!

1 Serving: Calories 110 (Calories from Fat 25); Total Fat 2.5g (Saturated Fat 1.5g; Trans Fat 0g); Cholesterol 10mg; Sodium 170mg; Total Carbohydrate 18g (Dietary Fiber 2g; Sugars 9g); Protein 3g   **% Daily Value:** Vitamin A 4%; Vitamin C 0%; Calcium 4%; Iron 4%   **Exchanges:** 1 Starch, ½ Fat   **Carbohydrate Choices:** 1

Cinnamon-Raisin Snack Mix

PREP TIME: **10 MINUTES** • START TO FINISH: **10 MINUTES** • **10 SERVINGS** (½ CUP EACH) • WHOLE GRAIN SERVING: ½

¼ cup sugar

1 teaspoon ground cinnamon

¼ cup butter or margarine

1½ cups Corn Chex® cereal

1½ cups Rice Chex® cereal

1½ cups Wheat Chex® cereal

½ cup raisins, sweetened dried cranberries or dried cherries

1   In small bowl, mix sugar and cinnamon; set aside.

2   In large microwavable bowl, microwave butter uncovered on High about 40 seconds, or until melted. Stir in cereals until evenly coated. Microwave uncovered 2 minutes, stirring after 1 minute.

3   Sprinkle half of the sugar mixture evenly over cereals; stir. Sprinkle with remaining sugar mixture; stir. Microwave uncovered 1 minute. Stir in raisins. Spread on paper towels to cool.

Betty Tip

This is such an easy snack to make, and because it's made in the microwave, it's a great choice to prepare in the summer. Scoop portions of it into small plastic bags and tuck into lunches, or bring along for any time you need an on-the-go snack.

1 Serving: Calories 170 (Calories from Fat 45); Total Fat 5g (Saturated Fat 3g; Trans Fat 0g); Cholesterol 10mg; Sodium 220mg; Total Carbohydrate 28g (Dietary Fiber 2g; Sugars 11g); Protein 2g **% Daily Value:** Vitamin A 8%; Vitamin C 2%; Calcium 6%; Iron 35% **Exchanges:** ½ Starch, 1½ Other Carbohydrate, 1 Fat **Carbohydrate Choices:** 2

Southwestern Popcorn Snack

PREP TIME: **10 MINUTES** • START TO FINISH: **10 MINUTES** • **8 SERVINGS** (1 CUP EACH) • WHOLE GRAIN SERVING: **½**

6 cups light microwave popcorn

2 cups Cheerios® cereal

2 tablespoons butter or margarine

½ teaspoon chili powder

¼ teaspoon ground cumin

¼ teaspoon garlic powder

2 tablespoons grated Parmesan cheese

1 In large bowl, mix popcorn and cereal; set aside.

2 In 6-inch nonstick skillet, heat butter, chili powder, cumin and garlic powder over low heat, stirring occasionally, until butter is melted.

3 Drizzle butter mixture over popcorn mixture; toss. Immediately sprinkle with cheese; toss. Serve warm.

Betty Tip

Popcorn and cereal are the two whole grains in this savory snack. If your popcorn has lost some of its crispness, spread it in a single layer in a shallow pan and heat in a 325°F oven for 5 to 10 minutes.

1 Serving: Calories 80 (Calories from Fat 40); Total Fat 4.5g (Saturated Fat 2.5g; Trans Fat 0g); Cholesterol 10mg; Sodium 150mg; Total Carbohydrate 9g (Dietary Fiber 1g; Sugars 0g); Protein 2g
% Daily Value: Vitamin A 6%; Vitamin C 0%; Calcium 4%; Iron 10% **Exchanges:** ½ Starch, 1 Fat
Carbohydrate Choices: ½

Campfire Popcorn Snack

PREP TIME: **5 MINUTES** • START TO FINISH: **30 MINUTES** • **20 SERVINGS** (½ CUP EACH) • WHOLE GRAIN SERVING: ½

6 cups popped light microwave
popcorn

4 cups Wheat Chex®, Corn
Chex® or Rice Chex® cereal

1 jar (7 oz) marshmallow creme

1 Heat oven to 350°F. Spray cookie sheet with cooking spray. In large bowl, mix popcorn and cereal; set aside.

2 In medium microwavable bowl, microwave marshmallow creme uncovered on High 1 minute; stir. Microwave about 1 minute longer or until melted; stir. Pour over popcorn mixture, stirring until evenly coated. Spread mixture on cookie sheet.

3 Bake 5 minutes; stir. Bake about 5 minutes longer or until coating is light golden brown. Spread on waxed paper. Cool about 15 minutes. Store in tightly covered container up to 2 weeks.

Betty Tip

The marshmallow creme adds sweetness to the popcorn and cereal without adding fat. The key to making good snack choices is to find the best-tasting snacks with healthy ingredients that are low in calories and still satisfy. This snack fills the bill!

1 Serving: Calories 90 (Calories from Fat 5); Total Fat 0.5g (Saturated Fat 0g; Trans Fat 0g); Cholesterol 0mg; Sodium 135mg; Total Carbohydrate 19g (Dietary Fiber 2g; Sugars 8g); Protein 2g **% Daily Value:** Vitamin A 2%; Vitamin C 0%; Calcium 2%; Iron 20% **Exchanges:** ½ Starch, 1 Other Carbohydrate **Carbohydrate Choices:** 1

Hiker's Trail Mix

PREP TIME: **5 MINUTES** • START TO FINISH: **5 MINUTES** • **8 SERVINGS** (ABOUT ½ CUP EACH) • WHOLE GRAIN SERVING: ½

1 cup roasted soy nuts

1 cup Wheat Chex® cereal

1 cup MultiGrain Cheerios®
    or Honey Nut Cheerios®
    cereal

1 cup raisins

½ cup candy-coated chocolate
    candies or chocolate chips

1 In large bowl, mix all ingredients.

2 Store in resealable plastic bag or tightly covered container.

Betty Tip

Soybeans have the highest-quality vegetable protein, considerably more than other legumes or nuts. Look for roasted soy nuts in the bulk-foods section at your local supermarket or food cooperative.

1 Serving: Calories 230 (Calories from Fat 50); Total Fat 6g (Saturated Fat 2g; Trans Fat 0g); Cholesterol 0mg; Sodium 120mg; Total Carbohydrate 37g (Dietary Fiber 4g; Sugars 20g); Protein 6g **% Daily Value:** Vitamin A 4%; Vitamin C 6%; Calcium 6%; Iron 30% **Exchanges:** 1 Starch, 1½ Other Carbohydrate, ½ High-Fat Meat **Carbohydrate Choices:** 2½

Crunchy Fruit Snack Mix

PREP TIME: **15 MINUTES** • START TO FINISH: **1 HOUR** • **10 SERVINGS** (ABOUT ¾ CUP EACH) • WHOLE GRAIN SERVING: ½

4 cups Total® Raisin Bran cereal

⅓ cup sliced almonds

1 bag (8 oz) dried mixed fruit (1½ cups), cut into ½-inch pieces

¼ cup packed brown sugar

2 tablespoons butter or margarine

2 teaspoons ground cinnamon

1 teaspoon ground ginger

1 Heat oven to 300°F. In large bowl, place cereal, almonds and fruit; set aside.

2 In 1-quart saucepan, heat brown sugar and butter over low heat, stirring occasionally, until butter is melted. Stir in cinnamon and ginger. Pour over cereal mixture; toss until evenly coated. Spread in ungreased 15 × 10 × 1-inch pan.

3 Bake 15 minutes, stirring twice. Spread on waxed paper. Cool about 30 minutes. Store in tightly covered container at room temperature.

Betty Tip

The cinnamon and ginger lend a spice twist to this amazing-tasting snack mix. Loaded with cereal, nuts and dried fruits, it stores well, so keep it on hand and munch on small amounts when you have a snack attack.

1 Serving: Calories 200 (Calories from Fat 40); Total Fat 4.5g (Saturated Fat 1.5g; Trans Fat 0g); Cholesterol 5mg; Sodium 120mg; Total Carbohydrate 38g (Dietary Fiber 4g; Sugars 24g); Protein 2g **% Daily Value:** Vitamin A 10%; Vitamin C 0%; Calcium 45%; Iron 45% **Exchanges:** ½ Starch, ½ Fruit, 1½ Other Carbohydrate, 1 Fat **Carbohydrate Choices:** 2½

Roasted Sesame and Honey Snack Mix

PREP TIME: **10 MINUTES** • START TO FINISH: **1 HOUR 25 MINUTES** • **20 SERVINGS** (½ CUP EACH) • WHOLE GRAIN SERVING: **½**

3 cups Wheat Chex® cereal

3 cups checkerboard-shaped pretzels

2 cups popped light microwave popcorn

1 cup sesame sticks

1 cup mixed nuts

¼ cup honey

3 tablespoons canola oil

2 tablespoons sesame seed, toasted, if desired*

✳ To quickly toast sesame seed, cook in an ungreased heavy skillet over medium-low heat 5 to 7 minutes, stirring frequently until browning begins, then stirring constantly until golden brown.

1 Heat oven to 275°F. In ungreased 15 × 10 × 1-inch pan, mix cereal, pretzels, popcorn, sesame sticks and nuts.

2 In small bowl, mix remaining ingredients. Pour over cereal mixture, stirring until evenly coated.

3 Bake 45 minutes, stirring occasionally. Spread on waxed paper. Cool about 30 minutes. Store in tightly covered container up to 1 week.

Betty Tip

Nuts contain a type of fat that is good for your heart. They make a great snack when you combine them with whole-grain cereal and low-fat popcorn.

1 Serving: Calories 150 (Calories from Fat 60); Total Fat 7g (Saturated Fat 1g; Trans Fat 0g); Cholesterol 0mg; Sodium 260mg; Total Carbohydrate 20g (Dietary Fiber 2g; Sugars 5g); Protein 3g **% Daily Value:** Vitamin A 2%; Vitamin C 0%; Calcium 2%; Iron 20% **Exchanges:** 1 Starch, 1½ Fat **Carbohydrate Choices:** 1

Soy Nut Snack Mix

PREP TIME: **10 MINUTES** • START TO FINISH: **1 HOUR 10 MINUTES** • **14 SERVINGS** (½ CUP EACH) • WHOLE GRAIN SERVING: **1**

2 tablespoons butter or
  margarine

1 tablespoon Worcestershire
  sauce

¾ teaspoon seasoned salt

½ teaspoon garlic powder

3 cups Wheat Chex® or
  Multi-Bran Chex® cereal

2 cups Cheerios® cereal

1 cup pretzel nuggets

1 cup salted-roasted soy nuts

1 Heat oven to 250°F. In large roasting pan, melt butter in oven. Stir Worcestershire sauce, seasoned salt and garlic powder into melted butter. Stir in remaining ingredients until all pieces are coated.

2 Bake 1 hour, stirring every 15 minutes. Spread on paper towels to cool. Store in airtight container.

Betty Tip

Just as a whole grain contains all three parts and nutrients of the grain, soy nuts contain all the parts and nutrients of the whole soybean.

1 Serving: Calories 130 (Calories from Fat 35); Total Fat 4g (Saturated Fat 1.5g; Trans Fat 0g); Cholesterol 0mg; Sodium 300mg; Total Carbohydrate 19g (Dietary Fiber 3g; Sugars 2g); Protein 4g
% Daily Value: Vitamin A 6%; Vitamin C 2%; Calcium 6%; Iron 30% **Exchanges:** ½ Starch, ½ Other Carbohydrate, ½ High-Fat Meat **Carbohydrate Choices:** 1

Sugar 'n' Spice Snack

PREP TIME: **10 MINUTES** • START TO FINISH: **1 HOUR 15 MINUTES** • **14 SERVINGS** (ABOUT ¾ CUP EACH) • WHOLE GRAIN SERVING: **½**

2 cups Wheat Chex® cereal

2 cups Apple Cinnamon
 Cheerios® cereal

1½ cups Cheerios® cereal

3 cups original flavor horn-
 shaped corn snacks

1½ cups dry-roasted peanuts

2 egg whites

2 tablespoons orange juice
 or water

1 cup sugar

1 teaspoon ground cinnamon

1   Heat oven to 300°F. Grease 15 × 10 × 1-inch pan with shortening or cooking spray.

2   In large bowl, mix cereals, corn snacks and peanuts. In small bowl, beat egg whites, orange juice, sugar and cinnamon with wire whisk or hand beater until foamy. Pour over cereal mixture, stirring until evenly coated. Spread in pan.

3   Bake 45 to 50 minutes, stirring every 15 minutes, until light brown and crisp. Cool completely, about 15 minutes. Store in airtight container.

Betty Tip

This recipe gives you the goodness of whole grains from the cereal, and protein and good fat from the nuts. If you'd like to add a little more crunch, you can stir in 1 cup of small pretzel twists before baking.

1 Serving: Calories 250 (Calories from Fat 90); Total Fat 10g (Saturated Fat 2.5g; Trans Fat 0g); Cholesterol 0mg; Sodium 300mg; Total Carbohydrate 34g (Dietary Fiber 3g; Sugars 19g); Protein 6g
% Daily Value: Vitamin A 4%; Vitamin C 4%; Calcium 6%; Iron 25% **Exchanges:** 1 Starch, 1 Other Carbohydrate, ½ High-Fat Meat, 1 Fat **Carbohydrate Choices:** 2

Hearty Munch Mix

PREP TIME: **5 MINUTES** • START TO FINISH: **5 MINUTES** • **10 SERVINGS** (ABOUT ¾ CUP EACH) • WHOLE GRAIN SERVING: ½

2 cups Cheerios® cereal

2 cups MultiGrain Cheerios® cereal

2 cups pretzel nuggets

½ cup yogurt-covered raisins

1 bag (7 oz) diced dried fruit and raisin mixture

In medium bowl, mix all ingredients.

Betty Tip

Make it an apple-cinnamon or honey-nut snack by using Apple Cinnamon, Honey Nut or other varieties of Cheerios® cereal. Serve this snack in ice cream cones for a fun and good-for-you after-school snack.

1 Serving: Calories 170 (Calories from Fat 25); Total Fat 2.5g (Saturated Fat 1.5g; Trans Fat 0g); Cholesterol 0mg; Sodium 230mg; Total Carbohydrate 35g (Dietary Fiber 3g; Sugars 18g); Protein 2g **% Daily Value:** Vitamin A 8%; Vitamin C 8%; Calcium 6%; Iron 35% **Exchanges:** 1 Starch, 1 Other Carbohydrate, ½ Fat **Carbohydrate Choices:** 2

Caramel Corn Crunch

PREP TIME: **15 MINUTES** • START TO FINISH: **30 MINUTES** • **12 SERVINGS** (ABOUT 1 CUP EACH) • WHOLE GRAIN SERVING: ½

6 cups popped light microwave popcorn

5 cups Cheerios® cereal

½ cup honey-roasted peanuts

¼ cup butter or margarine

6 tablespoons packed brown sugar

2 tablespoons light corn syrup

¼ teaspoon vanilla

1   In large microwavable bowl, mix popcorn, cereal and peanuts; set aside.

2   In medium microwavable bowl, microwave butter, brown sugar, corn syrup and vanilla uncovered on High about 2 minutes, stirring after 1 minute, until mixture is boiling. Pour over popcorn mixture, stirring until evenly coated.

3   Microwave popcorn mixture uncovered on High 5 to 6 minutes, stirring and scraping bowl after every minute. Spread on waxed paper. Cool about 15 minutes, stirring occasionally to break up. Store in tightly covered container.

Betty Tip

Kids love this caramel corn treat for the flavor and fun of it. You'll know that it's really good for them because both popcorn and cereal are whole grains. So let them snack away!

1 Serving: Calories 180 (Calories from Fat 80); Total Fat 8g (Saturated Fat 3g; Trans Fat 0g); Cholesterol 10mg; Sodium 180mg; Total Carbohydrate 22g (Dietary Fiber 2g; Sugars 9g); Protein 3g **% Daily Value:** Vitamin A 6%; Vitamin C 2%; Calcium 6%; Iron 20% **Exchanges:** 1 Starch, ½ Other Carbohydrate, 1½ Fat **Carbohydrate Choices:** 1½

dinners in 30 minutes

Mediterranean Shrimp with Bulgur
Page 118

4

Couscous, Corn and Lima Bean Sauté

PREP TIME: **20 MINUTES** • START TO FINISH: **25 MINUTES** • **6 SERVINGS** (1²/₃ CUPS EACH) • WHOLE GRAIN SERVING: **1½**

1 tablespoon butter or
    margarine
1 large onion, chopped (1 cup)
1 clove garlic, finely chopped
1 box (11 oz) whole wheat
    couscous
1 box (10 oz) frozen whole
    kernel corn, thawed
2 boxes (9 oz each) frozen baby
    lima beans, thawed
2 cups water
1 tablespoon chopped fresh
    or 1 teaspoon dried thyme
    leaves
1 teaspoon salt
⅓ cup slivered almonds,
    toasted (page 17)

1 In 12-inch skillet, melt butter over medium-high heat. Add onion and garlic; cook about 2 minutes, stirring occasionally, until onion is crisp-tender.

2 Stir in remaining ingredients except almonds. Heat to boiling over high heat. Remove from heat; let stand 5 minutes. Fluff before serving. Sprinkle with almonds.

Betty Tip

This recipe goes together in just minutes, thanks to whole wheat couscous, a whole grain that has already been cooked and dried. All you do is add water and veggies, heat to boiling, let stand and fluff. Now that's a real time savings!

1 Serving: Calories 390 (Calories from Fat 60); Total Fat 6g (Saturated Fat 1.5g; Trans Fat 0g); Cholesterol 5mg; Sodium 470mg; Total Carbohydrate 69g (Dietary Fiber 11g; Sugars 4g); Protein 15g
% Daily Value: Vitamin A 6%; Vitamin C 15%; Calcium 8%; Iron 20%   **Exchanges:** 4 Starch, 2 Vegetable, ½ Fat   **Carbohydrate Choices:** 4½

Asian Stir-Fry with Millet

PREP TIME: **10 MINUTES** • START TO FINISH: **30 MINUTES** • **6 SERVINGS** (1⅔ CUPS EACH) • WHOLE GRAIN SERVING: ½

2¼ cups reduced-sodium chicken broth

1 cup uncooked millet

2 bags (1 lb each) frozen broccoli, red peppers, onions and mushrooms (or other combination), thawed, drained

1⅓ cups apple juice

¼ cup reduced-sodium soy sauce

2 tablespoons cornstarch

½ teaspoon ground ginger

2 cups cut-up cooked chicken or turkey

1 In 2-quart saucepan, heat broth to boiling; reduce heat. Stir in millet. Cover; simmer 20 minutes.

2 Meanwhile, spray 12-inch skillet with cooking spray; heat over medium-high heat. Add vegetables and ⅓ cup of the apple juice. Cover; cook over medium heat 2 to 3 minutes or until vegetables are crisp-tender.

3 In small bowl, mix remaining 1 cup apple juice, the soy sauce, cornstarch and ginger. Gradually stir juice mixture into vegetable mixture. Heat to boiling, stirring constantly. Boil and stir 1 minute.

4 Stir chicken into vegetable mixture; cook about 2 minutes or until thoroughly heated. Toss with cooked millet.

Betty Tip

While millet may seem new, it has been around for centuries. It's delicious, plus it cooks in a short time.

1 Serving: Calories 310 (Calories from Fat 45); Total Fat 5g (Saturated Fat 1g; Trans Fat 0g); Cholesterol 40mg; Sodium 970mg; Total Carbohydrate 44g (Dietary Fiber 7g; Sugars 9g); Protein 22g **% Daily Value:** Vitamin A 30%; Vitamin C 50%; Calcium 6%; Iron 20% **Exchanges:** 1 Starch, 1½ Other Carbohydrate, 1½ Vegetable, 2 Lean Meat **Carbohydrate Choices:** 3

Skillet Shrimp and Veggie Dinner

PREP TIME: **30 MINUTES** • START TO FINISH: **30 MINUTES** • **4 SERVINGS** • WHOLE GRAIN SERVING: **2**

2½ cups chicken broth

1½ cups uncooked bulgur wheat

1 teaspoon lemon-pepper seasoning

1 medium green or red bell pepper, chopped (1 cup)

2 medium carrots, thinly sliced (1 cup)

1 jar (2.5 oz) sliced mushrooms, undrained

½ lb cooked deveined peeled medium shrimp, thawed if frozen

1 teaspoon grated lemon peel

1　In 2-quart saucepan, heat broth to boiling. Stir in remaining ingredients except shrimp and lemon peel. Heat to boiling.

2　Reduce heat. Cover; simmer 12 minutes (do not lift cover or stir).

3　Stir in shrimp and lemon peel. Cook until thoroughly heated.

Betty Tip

Surprise—whole grains don't have to take a long time to make. Because it's been precooked, bulgur wheat cooks in only 12 minutes. You can vary the color combo in this delightful dish by using red, orange and yellow bell peppers when they're in season.

1 Serving: Calories 280 (Calories from Fat 15); Total Fat 1.5g (Saturated Fat 0g; Trans Fat 0g); Cholesterol 110mg; Sodium 670mg; Total Carbohydrate 46g (Dietary Fiber 11g; Sugars 3g); Protein 21g **% Daily Value:** Vitamin A 80%; Vitamin C 20%; Calcium 8%; Iron 20% **Exchanges:** 2 Starch, 1 Other Carbohydrate, 2 Very Lean Meat **Carbohydrate Choices:** 3

Lemon-Pepper Fish Fillet Sandwiches

PREP TIME: **15 MINUTES** • START TO FINISH: **15 MINUTES** • **4 SANDWICHES** • WHOLE GRAIN SERVING: **2**

2 tablespoons whole-grain yellow cornmeal

2 tablespoons all-purpose flour

1 teaspoon seasoned salt

½ teaspoon lemon-pepper seasoning

1 tablespoon canola oil

2 walleye fillets (about 6 oz each), each cut crosswise in half

¼ cup tartar sauce

4 100% whole wheat or rye sandwich buns, toasted

1 cup shredded lettuce

1 In shallow bowl, mix cornmeal, flour, seasoned salt and lemon-pepper seasoning.

2 In 12-inch nonstick skillet, heat oil over medium-high heat. Coat fish fillets with flour mixture. Cook in oil 4 to 6 minutes, turning once, until fish flakes easily with fork.

3 Spread tartar sauce on cut sides of toasted buns. Layer lettuce and fish fillets in buns.

Betty Tip

Why not try a different type of fish instead of the walleye? Tilapia is another mild white fish that is delicious in this recipe.

1 Sandwich: Calories 330 (Calories from Fat 130); Total Fat 14g (Saturated Fat 2g; Trans Fat 0g); Cholesterol 50mg; Sodium 930mg; Total Carbohydrate 29g (Dietary Fiber 2g; Sugars 3g); Protein 21g **% Daily Value:** Vitamin A 2%; Vitamin C 0%; Calcium 6%; Iron 10% **Exchanges:** 1½ Starch, ½ Other Carbohydrate, 2 Very Lean Meat, 2½ Fat **Carbohydrate Choices:** 2

Rush-Hour Tuna Melts

PREP TIME: **10 MINUTES** • START TO FINISH: **20 MINUTES** • **4 SERVINGS** (2 SANDWICHES EACH) • WHOLE GRAIN SERVING: **2**

1 can (6 oz) white tuna in water, drained, flaked

¾ cup chopped celery

2 tablespoons finely chopped onion

½ teaspoon grated lemon peel, if desired

⅓ cup reduced-fat mayonnaise or salad dressing

4 100% whole wheat English muffins, split, lightly toasted

8 slices tomato

1 cup shredded reduced-fat Cheddar or Monterey Jack cheese (4 oz)

1 Heat oven to 350°F. In medium bowl, mix tuna, celery, onion, lemon peel and mayonnaise.

2 Spread about 3 tablespoons tuna mixture on each English muffin half. Top each with tomato slice; sprinkle with cheese. Place on ungreased cookie sheet.

3 Bake 8 to 10 minutes or until cheese is melted and sandwiches are thoroughly heated.

Betty Tip

It's never too early to include kids in healthy eating so they learn good habits from the start. Talk to them about whole grains, and let them make good choices. Having the kids help plan and prepare dinner increases their interest in foods and what they eat—get them going on these yummy sandwiches.

1 Serving: Calories 310 (Calories from Fat 90); Total Fat 10g (Saturated Fat 2.5g; Trans Fat 0g); Cholesterol 25mg; Sodium 970mg; Total Carbohydrate 31g (Dietary Fiber 5g; Sugars 6g); Protein 23g **% Daily Value:** Vitamin A 10%; Vitamin C 4%; Calcium 40%; Iron 15% **Exchanges:** 2 Starch, 2½ Very Lean Meat, 1½ Fat **Carbohydrate Choices:** 2

Pizza Burgers

PREP TIME: **20 MINUTES** • START TO FINISH: **20 MINUTES** • **6 SANDWICHES** • WHOLE GRAIN SERVING: **1**

1 lb extra-lean (at least 90%)
   ground beef

1 medium onion, chopped
   (½ cup)

1 small green bell pepper,
   chopped (½ cup)

1 jar (14 oz) pepperoni-flavored
   or regular pizza sauce

½ cup sliced ripe olives

6 100% whole wheat burger
   buns, split

¾ cup shredded pizza cheese
   blend (3 oz)

1   In 10-inch skillet, cook beef, onion and bell pepper over medium heat 8 to 10 minutes, stirring occasionally, until beef is thoroughly cooked; drain.

2   Stir pizza sauce and olives into beef. Heat to boiling, stirring occasionally.

3   Spoon about ½ cup beef mixture on bottom half of each bun. Immediately sprinkle each with 2 tablespoons of the cheese; add tops of buns. Serve immediately, or let stand about 2 minutes until cheese is melted.

Betty Tip
To up your servings of whole grains every day, choose whole wheat bread and buns.

1 Sandwich: Calories 300 (Calories from Fat 110); Total Fat 13g (Saturated Fat 5g; Trans Fat 1g); Cholesterol 55mg; Sodium 740mg; Total Carbohydrate 25g (Dietary Fiber 4g; Sugars 8g); Protein 23g **% Daily Value:** Vitamin A 6%; Vitamin C 10%; Calcium 15%; Iron 25% **Exchanges:** 1½ Starch, 2½ Lean Meat, 1 Fat **Carbohydrate Choices:** 1½

Broiled Dijon Burgers

PREP TIME: **20 MINUTES** • START TO FINISH: **20 MINUTES** • **6 SANDWICHES** • WHOLE GRAIN SERVING: **2**

1 egg

2 tablespoons milk

2 teaspoons Dijon mustard

¼ teaspoon salt

⅛ teaspoon pepper

1 cup soft bread crumbs
   (about 2 slices bread)

1 small onion, finely chopped
   (¼ cup)

1 lb extra-lean (at least 90%)
   ground beef

6 100% whole wheat burger
   buns, split, toasted

1   Set oven control to broil. Spray broiler pan rack with cooking spray.

2   In medium bowl, mix egg, milk, mustard, salt and pepper. Stir in bread crumbs and onion. Stir in beef. Shape mixture into 6 patties, each about ½ inch thick.

3   Place patties on rack in broiler pan. Broil with tops about 5 inches from heat for about 10 minutes for medium, turning once, until meat thermometer inserted in center reads 160°F. Serve burgers on buns.

Betty Tip

Even small changes can make a difference, so add whole grains whenever you can. Use whole-grain bread when making the bread crumbs, and serve on whole wheat hamburger buns.

1 Sandwich: Calories 270 (Calories from Fat 80); Total Fat 9g (Saturated Fat 3g; Trans Fat 1g); Cholesterol 85mg; Sodium 470mg; Total Carbohydrate 25g (Dietary Fiber 3g; Sugars 5g); Protein 21g **% Daily Value:** Vitamin A 0%; Vitamin C 0%; Calcium 6%; Iron 20% **Exchanges:** 1½ Starch, 2½ Lean Meat **Carbohydrate Choices:** 1½

Grilled Mushroom-Swiss Veggie Burgers

PREP TIME: **20 MINUTES** • START TO FINISH: **20 MINUTES** • **4 SERVINGS** • WHOLE GRAIN SERVING: **2**

4 frozen soy-protein vegetable
burgers

1 jar (4.5 oz) sliced mushrooms,
drained

4 slices (about 1 oz each) Swiss
cheese

¼ cup reduced-fat mayonnaise
or salad dressing

4 100% whole wheat burger
buns

4 tomato slices

4 lettuce leaves

Ketchup and mustard, if desired

1 Heat gas or charcoal grill. Place burgers on grill. Cover; cook over medium heat 6 to 9 minutes, turning once, until thoroughly heated.

2 Divide mushrooms evenly among burgers; top with cheese. Cover; grill 1 to 2 minutes longer or until cheese is melted.

3 Spread 1 tablespoon mayonnaise on each bun. Serve burgers on buns with tomatoes, lettuce, ketchup and mustard.

Betty Tip

If you haven't tried veggie burgers lately, you're in for a treat. Veggie burgers come in many flavors, from Cajun-spiced to classic grilled. Choose your favorite low-fat version. Team these burgers with classic picnic fare: carrot and celery sticks, fresh-cut melon and lemonade.

1 Serving: Calories 340 (Calories from Fat 110); Total Fat 12g (Saturated Fat 3g; Trans Fat 0g); Cholesterol 15mg; Sodium 890mg; Total Carbohydrate 31g (Dietary Fiber 6g; Sugars 8g); Protein 27g **% Daily Value:** Vitamin A 25%; Vitamin C 4%; Calcium 40%; Iron 20% **Exchanges:** 1½ Starch, ½ Other Carbohydrate, 3 Lean Meat, ½ Fat **Carbohydrate Choices:** 2

Classic Chicken Panini

PREP TIME: **20 MINUTES** • START TO FINISH: **20 MINUTES** • **4 SANDWICHES** • WHOLE GRAIN SERVING: **2**

4 boneless skinless chicken breasts (4 oz each)

½ teaspoon salt-free seasoning blend

¼ cup reduced-fat mayonnaise or salad dressing

2 teaspoons white or flavored vinegar

½ teaspoon garlic powder

4 100% whole wheat English muffins, split

4 slices (¾ oz each) mozzarella cheese

4 thin slices red onion

1 plum (Roma) tomato, cut into 8 slices

1   Heat closed medium-size contact grill for 5 minutes. Sprinkle chicken with seasoning blend. Place chicken on grill. Close grill; cook 4 to 5 minutes or until juice of chicken is clear when center of thickest part is cut (165°F).

2   Meanwhile, in small bowl, mix mayonnaise, vinegar and garlic powder. Spread on English muffin halves. Place chicken on bottoms of English muffins. Top with cheese, onion, tomato and tops of muffins.

3   Place sandwiches on grill. Close grill, pressing to flatten sandwiches; cook 2 to 3 minutes or until sandwiches are toasted.

Betty Tip

Try this tasty sandwich with other types of cheese, such as reduced-fat Swiss, provolone or Cheddar.

1 Sandwich: Calories 400 (Calories from Fat 130); Total Fat 14g (Saturated Fat 4.5g; Trans Fat 0g); Cholesterol 85mg; Sodium 700mg; Total Carbohydrate 31g (Dietary Fiber 5g; Sugars 5g); Protein 37g
% Daily Value: Vitamin A 6%; Vitamin C 0%; Calcium 35%; Iron 15% **Exchanges:** 1½ Starch, ½ Other Carbohydrate, 4½ Very Lean Meat, 2 Fat **Carbohydrate Choices:** 2

Beef, Lettuce and Tomato Wraps

PREP TIME: **30 MINUTES** • START TO FINISH: **30 MINUTES** • **4 SERVINGS** • WHOLE GRAIN SERVING: ½

1 tablespoon plus 1½ teaspoons chili powder

2 teaspoons dried oregano leaves

1 teaspoon ground cumin

1 teaspoon salt

1 lb beef top sirloin steak, about ¾ inch thick

4 whole wheat tortillas (6 to 8 inch)

¾ cup reduced-fat sour cream

1 tablespoon prepared horseradish

4 cups shredded lettuce

1 large tomato, chopped (1 cup)

1   In small bowl, mix chili powder, oregano, cumin and salt. Rub mixture on both sides of beef. Let stand 10 minutes at room temperature.

2   Set oven control to broil. Place beef on rack in broiler pan. Broil with top 3 to 4 inches from heat for about 10 minutes for medium doneness, turning once, or until desired doneness. Cut into ⅛-inch slices.

3   Warm tortillas as directed on package. In small bowl, mix sour cream and horseradish. Spread 3 tablespoons horseradish mixture over each tortilla; top each with 1 cup of the lettuce and ¼ cup of the tomato. Top with beef. Wrap tortillas around filling.

Betty Tip

Your supermarket is likely offering many whole-grain options. Look for whole wheat tortillas, which are a great alternative to the white ones. Besides being a whole grain, they have more flavor and texture.

1 Serving: Calories 280 (Calories from Fat 90); Total Fat 10g (Saturated Fat 5g; Trans Fat 0g); Cholesterol 80mg; Sodium 790mg; Total Carbohydrate 17g (Dietary Fiber 4g; Sugars 5g); Protein 30g **% Daily Value:** Vitamin A 30%; Vitamin C 20%; Calcium 10%; Iron 25% **Exchanges:** 1 Starch, 4 Very Lean Meat, 1½ Fat **Carbohydrate Choices:** 1

Beef and Kasha Mexicana

PREP TIME: **10 MINUTES** • START TO FINISH: **25 MINUTES** • **6 SERVINGS** (1⅓ CUPS EACH) • WHOLE GRAIN SERVING: ½

1 lb extra-lean (at least 90%) ground beef

1 small onion, chopped (½ cup)

1 cup uncooked buckwheat kernels or groats (kasha)

1 can (14.5 oz) diced tomatoes, undrained

1 can (4.5 oz) chopped green chiles, undrained

1 package (1 oz) 40%-less-sodium taco seasoning mix

2 cups frozen whole kernel corn (from 1-lb bag), thawed

1½ cups water

1 cup shredded reduced-fat Cheddar cheese (4 oz)

2 tablespoons chopped fresh cilantro, if desired

2 tablespoons sliced ripe olives, if desired

1 In 12-inch skillet, cook ground beef and onion over medium-high heat 5 to 7 minutes, stirring occasionally, until beef is thoroughly cooked; drain. Stir in kasha until kernels are moistened by beef mixture.

2 Stir in tomatoes, chiles, taco seasoning mix, corn and water. Heat to boiling. Cover; reduce heat to low. Simmer 5 to 7 minutes, stirring occasionally, until kasha is tender.

3 Sprinkle cheese over kasha mixture. Cover; cook 2 to 3 minutes or until cheese is melted. Sprinkle with cilantro and olives.

Betty Tip

This tasty main dish combines whole-grain kasha with beef and uses familiar Mexican ingredients. It's a great transition recipe, when you're just starting to eat grains. You can also use this mixture as a filling for tortillas.

1 Serving: Calories 300 (Calories from Fat 80); Total Fat 9g (Saturated Fat 3.5g; Trans Fat 0g); Cholesterol 50mg; Sodium 990mg; Total Carbohydrate 33g (Dietary Fiber 5g; Sugars 5g); Protein 23g **% Daily Value:** Vitamin A 15%; Vitamin C 10%; Calcium 20%; Iron 25% **Exchanges:** 2 Starch, 2½ Lean Meat **Carbohydrate Choices:** 2

Italian Frittata with Vinaigrette Tomatoes

PREP TIME: **10 MINUTES** • START TO FINISH: **30 MINUTES** • **5 SERVINGS** • WHOLE GRAIN SERVING: ½

1 can (14 oz) chicken broth

¾ cup uncooked bulgur wheat

1 medium zucchini, sliced, slices cut in half crosswise (1½ cups)

1 cup sliced fresh mushrooms (3 oz)

1 small red bell pepper, chopped (½ cup)

1 small onion, chopped (¼ cup)

½ teaspoon dried oregano leaves

½ teaspoon dried basil leaves

6 eggs

⅓ cup milk

¼ teaspoon salt

¼ teaspoon pepper

½ cup shredded mozzarella cheese (2 oz)

3 medium plum (Roma) tomatoes, chopped, drained (1 cup)

2 tablespoons balsamic vinaigrette dressing

1   Heat oven to 350°F. In 12-inch ovenproof nonstick skillet, heat broth to boiling over high heat. Stir in bulgur; reduce heat to low. Top bulgur evenly with zucchini, mushrooms, bell pepper and onion. Sprinkle with oregano and basil. Cover; cook 12 minutes. Fluff bulgur with spatula, mixing with vegetables.

2   Meanwhile, in medium bowl, beat eggs, milk, salt and pepper with wire whisk until well blended. Pour egg mixture evenly over bulgur mixture. Increase heat to medium-low. Cover; cook 5 minutes.

3   Remove cover; sprinkle with cheese. Bake uncovered 5 to 7 minutes or until sharp knife inserted in center of egg mixture comes out clean.

4   Meanwhile, in medium microwavable bowl, mix tomatoes and dressing. Microwave uncovered on High 30 seconds to blend flavors.

5   Cut frittata into wedges (bulgur will form a "crust" on the bottom; use spatula to lift wedge out of skillet). Top with tomato mixture.

Betty Tip

Bulgur adds an extra chewiness and heartiness to this fantastic frittata, and kids love it! To substitute for the oregano and basil, you can use 1 teaspoon Italian seasoning.

1 Serving: Calories 264 (Calories from Fat 108); Total Fat 12g (Saturated Fat 4g; Trans Fat 0g); Cholesterol 264mg; Sodium 684mg; Total Carbohydrate 24g (Dietary Fiber 5g; Sugars 6g); Protein 17g **% Daily Value:** Vitamin A 24%; Vitamin C 36%; Calcium 18%; Iron 10%   **Exchanges:** 1 Starch, 1 Vegetable, 1 Medium-Fat Meat, 1 Fat   **Carbohydrate Choices:** 1½

Creamy Alfredo-Turkey Skillet Dinner

PREP TIME: **25 MINUTES** • START TO FINISH: **25 MINUTES** • **4 SERVINGS** (1½ CUPS EACH) • WHOLE GRAIN SERVING: **1**

2 cups uncooked whole wheat rotini pasta (6 oz)

1 lb lean ground turkey

1 teaspoon Italian seasoning

¼ teaspoon salt

3 cups firmly packed fresh spinach leaves

1 container (10 oz) refrigerated reduced-fat Alfredo pasta sauce

1 can (14.5 oz) petite diced tomatoes, undrained

¼ cup shredded Parmesan cheese (1 oz)

1   In 2-quart saucepan, cook and drain pasta as directed on package, omitting salt.

2   Meanwhile, in 12-inch nonstick skillet, cook turkey, Italian seasoning and salt over medium-high heat 6 to 8 minutes, stirring occasionally, until turkey is no longer pink; drain.

3   Stir spinach into turkey. Cook uncovered over medium heat 2 to 3 minutes, stirring occasionally, until spinach is wilted. Stir in pasta sauce and tomatoes. Cook 2 to 3 minutes, stirring occasionally, until thoroughly heated. Stir in pasta.

4   Sprinkle with cheese; reduce heat to low. Cover; cook about 5 minutes or until cheese is melted.

Betty Tip

Whole grains have many health benefits. Studies show that incorporating whole grains into your diet may help reduce the risk of heart disease, stroke, cancer, diabetes and obesity.

1 Serving: Calories 470 (Calories from Fat 150); Total Fat 17g (Saturated Fat 8g; Trans Fat 0g); Cholesterol 105mg; Sodium 800mg; Total Carbohydrate 41g (Dietary Fiber 5g; Sugars 6g); Protein 39g **% Daily Value:** Vitamin A 50%; Vitamin C 15%; Calcium 30%; Iron 25% **Exchanges:** 2 Starch, ½ Other Carbohydrate, 1 Vegetable, 4½ Very Lean Meat, 2½ Fat **Carbohydrate Choices:** 3

Chicken and Vegetables with Quinoa

PREP TIME: **25 MINUTES** • START TO FINISH: **25 MINUTES** • **4 SERVINGS** (1 CUP STIR-FRY AND 1 CUP QUINOA EACH) •
WHOLE GRAIN SERVING: **2½**

1⅓ cups uncooked quinoa

2⅔ cups water

⅔ cup chicken broth

2 cups 1-inch pieces fresh green beans

½ cup ready-to-eat baby-cut carrots, cut in half lengthwise

1 tablespoon olive oil

½ lb boneless skinless chicken breasts, cut into bite-size pieces

½ cup bite-size strips red bell pepper

½ cup sliced fresh mushrooms

½ teaspoon dried rosemary leaves

¼ teaspoon salt

2 cloves garlic, finely chopped

1   Rinse quinoa thoroughly by placing in a fine-mesh strainer and holding under cold running water until water runs clear; drain well.

2   In 2-quart saucepan, heat water to boiling. Add quinoa; return to boiling. Reduce heat to low. Cover; cook 12 to 16 minutes or until liquid is absorbed.

3   Meanwhile, in 12-inch nonstick skillet, heat broth to boiling over high heat. Add green beans and carrots. Reduce heat to medium-high. Cover; cook 5 to 7 minutes or until vegetables are crisp-tender.

4   Stir oil, chicken, bell pepper, mushrooms, rosemary, salt and garlic into vegetables. Cook over medium-high heat 8 to 9 minutes, stirring frequently, until chicken is no longer pink in center. Serve over quinoa.

Betty Tip

Quinoa, pronounced "KEEN-wa," was first grown in Peru. It contains all the amino acids, making it a complete protein—it is quick and easy to cook, making it a favorite grain. Quinoa's texture is light with a nutty flavor, perfect for main and side dishes.

1 Serving: Calories 350 (Calories from Fat 80); Total Fat 9g (Saturated Fat 1.5g; Trans Fat 0g); Cholesterol 35mg; Sodium 380mg; Total Carbohydrate 46g (Dietary Fiber 6g; Sugars 6g); Protein 22g
% Daily Value: Vitamin A 50%; Vitamin C 20%; Calcium 8%; Iron 35% **Exchanges:** 2 Starch, ½ Other Carbohydrate, 1 Vegetable, 2 Very Lean Meat, 1½ Fat **Carbohydrate Choices:** 3

Quinoa Pilaf with Salmon and Asparagus

PREP TIME: **30 MINUTES** • START TO FINISH: **30 MINUTES** • **4 SERVINGS** (1¾ CUPS EACH) • WHOLE GRAIN SERVING: **2**

1 cup uncooked quinoa

6 cups water

1 vegetable bouillon cube

1 lb salmon fillets

2 tablespoons butter or margarine

20 stalks fresh asparagus, cut diagonally into 2-inch pieces (2 cups)

4 medium green onions, sliced (¼ cup)

1 cup frozen sweet peas, thawed

½ cup halved grape tomatoes

½ cup vegetable or chicken broth

1 teaspoon lemon-pepper seasoning

2 teaspoons chopped fresh or ½ teaspoon dried dill weed

1 Rinse quinoa thoroughly by placing in a fine-mesh strainer and holding under cold running water until water runs clear; drain well.

2 In 2-quart saucepan, heat 2 cups of the water to boiling over high heat. Add quinoa; reduce heat to low. Cover; simmer 10 to 12 minutes or until water is absorbed.

3 Meanwhile, in 12-inch skillet, heat remaining 4 cups water and bouillon cube to boiling over high heat. Add salmon, skin side up; reduce heat to low. Cover; simmer 10 to 12 minutes or until fish flakes easily with fork. Remove with slotted spoon to plate; let cool. Discard water. Remove skin from salmon; break into large pieces.

4 Meanwhile, rinse and dry skillet. Melt butter in skillet over medium heat. Add asparagus; cook 5 minutes, stirring frequently. Stir in onions; cook 1 minute, stirring frequently. Stir in peas, tomatoes and broth; cook 1 minute.

5 Gently stir quinoa, salmon, lemon-pepper seasoning and dill weed into asparagus mixture. Cover; cook about 2 minutes or until thoroughly heated.

Betty Tip

This main dish tastes as good as it looks and will be requested again and again. Vegetable broth and chicken broth are available in convenient 32-ounce resealable cartons. Cooking grains in broth adds flavor and pizzazz to your recipes.

1 Serving: Calories 420 (Calories from Fat 140); Total Fat 15g (Saturated Fat 6g; Trans Fat 0g); Cholesterol 90mg; Sodium 650mg; Total Carbohydrate 37g (Dietary Fiber 5g; Sugars 6g); Protein 34g
% Daily Value: Vitamin A 35%; Vitamin C 20%; Calcium 8%; Iron 30% **Exchanges:** 1½ Starch, ½ Other Carbohydrate, 1 Vegetable, 4 Lean Meat, ½ Fat **Carbohydrate Choices:** 2½

Mediterranean Shrimp with Bulgur

PREP TIME: **25 MINUTES** • START TO FINISH: **25 MINUTES** • **6 SERVINGS** (1⅓ CUPS EACH) • WHOLE GRAIN SERVING: **1**

2 cups water

1 cup uncooked bulgur wheat

2 teaspoons olive oil

1 medium onion, chopped (½ cup)

¼ cup dry white wine or nonalcoholic wine

2 cans (14.5 oz each) diced tomatoes with basil, oregano and garlic, undrained

3 tablespoons chopped fresh parsley

1 tablespoon capers, drained

¼ teaspoon freshly ground black pepper

⅛ teaspoon crushed red pepper flakes

1 lb uncooked small (30 to 40 count) shrimp, peeled, deveined

½ cup crumbled reduced-fat feta cheese (2 oz)

1 In 2-quart saucepan, heat water to boiling. Add bulgur; reduce heat to low. Cover; simmer about 12 minutes or until water is absorbed.

2 Meanwhile, in 12-inch skillet, heat oil over medium heat. Add onion; cook about 4 minutes, stirring occasionally, until tender. Stir in wine; cook 1 minute, stirring frequently.

3 Stir tomatoes, 1½ tablespoons of the parsley, the capers, black pepper and red pepper flakes into onion. Cook 3 minutes. Stir in shrimp. Cover; cook 4 to 5 minutes or until shrimp are pink.

4 Stir cooked bulgur into shrimp mixture. Sprinkle with cheese. Cover; cook 2 minutes. Sprinkle with remaining 1½ tablespoons parsley.

Betty Tip

If you cannot find diced tomatoes with basil, oregano and garlic, use plain diced tomatoes and add 1 teaspoon each of finely chopped fresh garlic, dried oregano and dried basil.

1 Serving: Calories 210 (Calories from Fat 35); Total Fat 4g (Saturated Fat 1.5g; Trans Fat 0g); Cholesterol 110mg; Sodium 480mg; Total Carbohydrate 25g (Dietary Fiber 6g; Sugars 4g); Protein 18g **% Daily Value:** Vitamin A 10%; Vitamin C 15%; Calcium 10%; Iron 20% **Exchanges:** 1 Starch, 1 Vegetable, 2 Very Lean Meat, ½ Fat **Carbohydrate Choices:** 1½

easy main dishes

Beef and Millet Stew in
Bread Bowls *Page 142*

Tabbouleh with Garbanzo Beans

PREP TIME: **15 MINUTES** • START TO FINISH: **1 HOUR 15 MINUTES** • **4 SERVINGS** • WHOLE GRAIN SERVING: **1**

Tabbouleh

1½ cups boiling water

¾ cup uncooked bulgur wheat

3 medium tomatoes, chopped (2¼ cups)

8 medium green onions, chopped (½ cup)

1 medium green bell pepper, chopped (1 cup)

1 cup chopped cucumber

¾ cup chopped fresh parsley

3 tablespoons chopped fresh or 1 tablespoon dried mint leaves, crushed

1 can (15 to 16 oz) garbanzo beans, drained

Lemon-Garlic Dressing

¼ cup lemon juice

1 tablespoon olive or vegetable oil

¾ teaspoon salt

¼ teaspoon pepper

3 cloves garlic, finely chopped

1 In medium bowl, pour boiling water over bulgur. Let stand 1 hour.

2 In tightly covered container, shake all dressing ingredients.

3 Drain any remaining water from bulgur. Stir remaining tabbouleh ingredients into bulgur. Pour dressing over tabbouleh; toss.

Betty Tip

Middle Eastern cuisine gives us many foods that are low in fat and high in flavor. A favorite from this region is tabbouleh, which features whole-grain bulgur wheat kernels that have been steamed, dried and crushed.

1 Serving: Calories 340 (Calories from Fat 60); Total Fat 7g (Saturated Fat 1g; Trans Fat 0g); Cholesterol 0mg; Sodium 600mg; Total Carbohydrate 56g (Dietary Fiber 14g; Sugars 6g); Protein 14g **% Daily Value:** Vitamin A 45%; Vitamin C 110%; Calcium 10%; Iron 25% **Exchanges:** 2½ Starch, 1 Other Carbohydrate, 1 Vegetable, ½ Very Lean Meat, 1 Fat **Carbohydrate Choices:** 4

Chicken and Veggies with Bulgur

PREP TIME: **25 MINUTES** • START TO FINISH: **30 MINUTES** • **4 SERVINGS** (1 CUP EACH) • WHOLE GRAIN SERVING: **1½**

2 cups chicken broth

1 cup uncooked bulgur wheat

½ teaspoon dried dill weed

½ teaspoon garlic salt

½ lb boneless skinless chicken breasts, cut into ¾-inch pieces

2 teaspoons canola oil

2½ cups thinly sliced zucchini or carrots (about 2 medium zucchini or 5 medium carrots)

1 medium onion, cut in half lengthwise, then cut crosswise into thin slices

1 In 1½-quart saucepan, heat broth to boiling. Stir in bulgur, dill weed and garlic salt. Reduce heat to low. Cover; simmer 20 to 25 minutes or until bulgur is tender. Remove from heat.

2 Meanwhile, spray 10-inch skillet with cooking spray; heat over medium-high heat. Add chicken; cook about 4 minutes, stirring frequently, until no longer pink in center. Remove chicken from skillet; keep warm.

3 Add oil to skillet; rotate skillet to coat with oil. Add zucchini and onion; cook about 4 to 5 minutes, stirring frequently, until vegetables are crisp-tender. Stir in chicken. Toss with cooked bulgur.

Betty Tip

Bulgur wheat is a great grain to serve for a weeknight dinner because it cooks in only 20 minutes. Make this satisfying chicken stir-fry more colorful by using a mixture of zucchini and carrots.

1 Serving: Calories 160 (Calories from Fat 45); Total Fat 5g (Saturated Fat 1g; Trans Fat 0g); Cholesterol 35mg; Sodium 900mg; Total Carbohydrate 12g (Dietary Fiber 3g; Sugars 3g); Protein 17g **% Daily Value:** Vitamin A 4%; Vitamin C 10%; Calcium 4%; Iron 6% **Exchanges:** ½ Starch, 1 Vegetable, 2 Very Lean Meat, ½ Fat **Carbohydrate Choices:** 1

Three-Grain Salad

PREP TIME: **25 MINUTES** • START TO FINISH: **3 HOURS 30 MINUTES** • **5 SERVINGS (1⅓ CUPS EACH)** •
WHOLE GRAIN SERVING: **1**

Salad

5½ cups water

1 cup uncooked wheat berries

⅓ cup uncooked long-grain
    brown rice

½ cup uncooked hulled or pearl
    barley

½ cup dried cherries or
    cranberries

¼ cup diced carrot

¼ cup diced celery

¼ cup chopped fresh parsley,
    if desired

1 medium unpeeled eating
    apple, chopped (1 cup)

4 medium green onions,
    chopped (¼ cup)

Sweet Red Onion Dressing

⅓ cup sugar

⅓ cup canola oil

⅓ cup cider vinegar

2 tablespoons grated red onion

2 teaspoons Worcestershire
    sauce

2 cloves garlic, finely chopped

1 In 2-quart saucepan, heat water and wheat berries to boiling. Reduce heat to low. Cover; simmer 10 minutes. Stir in brown rice and barley. Cover; simmer about 50 minutes longer or until grains are tender. Drain if necessary.

2 In small bowl, mix all dressing ingredients.

3 In large bowl, mix cooked grains and remaining salad ingredients. Pour dressing over salad; toss. Cover; refrigerate 1 to 2 hours or until chilled.

Betty Tip

You'll agree that this salad, made with three grains, is worth the time and effort to prepare. It has an amazing flavor that's even better the second day. And, when pomegranates are in season, the seeds make a great substitution for the cherries.

1 Serving: Calories 450 (Calories from Fat 140); Total Fat 16g (Saturated Fat 1.5g; Trans Fat 0g); Cholesterol 0mg; Sodium 50mg; Total Carbohydrate 71g (Dietary Fiber 8g; Sugars 26g); Protein 6g **% Daily Value:** Vitamin A 30%; Vitamin C 2%; Calcium 4%; Iron 10% **Exchanges:** 2 Starch, 2½ Other Carbohydrate, 3 Fat **Carbohydrate Choices:** 5

Crunchy Garlic Chicken Dinner

PREP TIME: **30 MINUTES** • START TO FINISH: **55 MINUTES** • **6 SERVINGS** • WHOLE GRAIN SERVING: **1½**

2 cups Country® Corn Flakes cereal

¼ cup butter or margarine, melted

2 tablespoons milk

1 tablespoon chopped fresh chives

½ teaspoon salt

½ teaspoon garlic powder

3 tablespoons chopped fresh parsley

½ teaspoon paprika

6 boneless skinless chicken breasts (about 1¾ lb)

1 box (11 oz) whole wheat couscous

2 cups water

1 tablespoon olive oil

1   Heat oven to 425°F. Spray 13 × 9-inch pan with cooking spray. Place cereal in resealable food-storage plastic bag or between sheets of waxed paper; crush with rolling pin. Set aside.

2   In shallow dish, mix 2 tablespoons of the butter, the milk, chives, salt and garlic powder. In another shallow dish, mix crushed cereal, parsley and paprika. Dip chicken into milk mixture, then coat lightly and evenly with cereal mixture. Place in pan. Drizzle with remaining 2 tablespoons butter.

3   Bake 20 to 25 minutes or until juice of chicken is clear when center of thickest part is cut (165°F).

4   Meanwhile, make couscous as directed on box for 5 servings, using water and oil. Serve chicken with couscous.

Betty Tip

Corn flakes make a crunchy, tasty coating for this savory chicken. Serving it with whole wheat couscous boosts the whole grain in this great-tasting main dish.

1 Serving: Calories 480 (Calories from Fat 140); Total Fat 15g (Saturated Fat 6g; Trans Fat 0.5g); Cholesterol 100mg; Sodium 420mg; Total Carbohydrate 48g (Dietary Fiber 5g; Sugars 0g); Protein 37g **% Daily Value:** Vitamin A 15%; Vitamin C 4%; Calcium 15%; Iron 30% **Exchanges:** 3 Starch, 4 Very Lean Meat, 2 Fat **Carbohydrate Choices:** 3

Chicken with Gingered Brown Rice

PREP TIME: **10 MINUTES** • START TO FINISH: **1 HOUR 10 MINUTES** • **4 SERVINGS** • WHOLE GRAIN SERVING: **1½**

1 cup uncooked long-grain brown rice

2¾ cups water

2 tablespoons orange juice

1 small onion, finely chopped (¼ cup)

3 tablespoons finely chopped crystallized ginger

2 tablespoons chopped fresh parsley or 2 teaspoons parsley flakes

¾ teaspoon chopped fresh or ¼ teaspoon dried thyme leaves

4 boneless skinless chicken breasts (about 1¼ lb)

3 tablespoons orange marmalade

1 tablespoon canola oil

1 Cook brown rice in water as directed on package, or see page 16; drain if necessary.

2 Heat oven to 350°F. Spray 8-inch square (2-quart) glass baking dish with cooking spray. In 2-quart saucepan, heat 1 tablespoon of the orange juice to boiling over medium heat. Cook onion in orange juice 1 to 2 minutes, stirring frequently, until crisp-tender. Stir in cooked rice, ginger, parsley, thyme and remaining 1 tablespoon orange juice.

3 Spoon rice mixture into baking dish. Place chicken breasts on rice mixture. In small bowl, mix marmalade and oil; brush over chicken.

4 Cover baking dish with foil; bake 25 minutes. Remove cover; bake 10 to 15 minutes longer or until juice of chicken is clear when center of thickest part is cut (165°F).

Betty Tip

The orange juice, marmalade, ginger and herbs add a wonderful flavor to this tasty chicken and long-grain rice dish.

1 Serving: Calories 440 (Calories from Fat 80); Total Fat 9g (Saturated Fat 2g; Trans Fat 0g); Cholesterol 85mg; Sodium 95mg; Total Carbohydrate 53g (Dietary Fiber 6g; Sugars 9g); Protein 35g **% Daily Value:** Vitamin A 4%; Vitamin C 6%; Calcium 4%; Iron 10% **Exchanges:** 2½ Starch, 1 Other Carbohydrate, 4 Very Lean Meat, 1 Fat **Carbohydrate Choices:** 3 ½

Wild Rice–Pecan Patties with Red Onion Chutney

PREP TIME: **40 MINUTES** • START TO FINISH: **40 MINUTES** • **5 SERVINGS** (2 PATTIES AND 2 TABLESPOONS CHUTNEY EACH) • WHOLE GRAIN SERVING: **½**

Chutney

1 tablespoon canola oil

1½ cups sliced red onion (1 large)

½ cup packed brown sugar

⅓ cup red wine vinegar

¼ cup diced dried fruit and raisin mixture

¼ teaspoon pumpkin pie spice

Patties

½ cup uncooked wild rice

1¼ cups water

1 cup soft bread crumbs (about 1½ slices bread)

⅓ cup chopped pecans

½ teaspoon garlic salt

3 eggs

1 jar (2.5 oz) mushroom pieces and stems, drained, finely chopped

1 jar (2 oz) diced pimientos, drained

2 tablespoons canola oil

1 In 2-quart saucepan, heat 1 tablespoon oil over medium heat. Cook onion in oil about 6 minutes, stirring frequently, until onion is tender. Stir in remaining chutney ingredients. Heat to boiling; reduce heat to low. Cook 20 to 25 minutes or until dried fruits are plump and mixture has thickened; remove from heat.

2 Meanwhile, cook wild rice in water as directed on package, or see page 16; drain if necessary. In large bowl, mix cooked wild rice and remaining patty ingredients except oil.

3 In 12-inch skillet, heat 2 tablespoons oil over medium heat. Scoop wild rice mixture by ⅓ cupfuls into skillet; flatten to ½ inch. Cook about 3 minutes on each side or until light brown. Remove patties from skillet; cover and keep warm while cooking remaining patties. Serve with chutney.

Betty Tip

You can make Wild Rice–Corn Patties. Just substitute ⅓ cup frozen (thawed) whole kernel corn for the pecans.

1 Serving: Calories 400 (Calories from Fat 150); Total Fat 17g (Saturated Fat 2g; Trans Fat 0g); Cholesterol 125mg; Sodium 260mg; Total Carbohydrate 52g (Dietary Fiber 4g; Sugars 29g); Protein 9g **% Daily Value:** Vitamin A 10%; Vitamin C 10%; Calcium 8%; Iron 10% **Exchanges:** 1½ Starch, 2 Other Carbohydrate, ½ Medium-Fat Meat, 2½ Fat **Carbohydrate Choices:** 3 ½

Creamy Chicken and Wild Rice Casserole

PREP TIME: **25 MINUTES** • START TO FINISH: **1 HOUR 55 MINUTES** • **4 SERVINGS** • WHOLE GRAIN SERVING: **1**

⅔ cup uncooked wild rice

1⅔ cups water

2 tablespoons water

1 medium stalk celery, chopped (½ cup)

1 medium onion, chopped (½ cup)

1 small red or green bell pepper, chopped (½ cup)

1 cup sliced mushrooms (about 3 oz)

1 can (10¾ oz) condensed cream of chicken soup

¾ cup milk

1 cup cut-up cooked chicken

¾ teaspoon chopped fresh or ¼ teaspoon dried thyme leaves

⅛ teaspoon pepper

1 can (8 oz) sliced water chestnuts, drained

1 Cook wild rice in 1⅔ cups water as directed on package, or see page 16; drain if necessary.

2 Heat oven to 350°F. In 2-quart saucepan, heat 2 tablespoons water to boiling. Cook celery, onion, bell pepper and mushrooms in water, stirring frequently, until crisp-tender; remove from heat.

3 Stir in soup and milk. Stir in cooked wild rice and remaining ingredients. Spoon into ungreased 2-quart casserole.

4 Cover; bake 30 to 40 minutes or until hot and bubbly.

Betty Tip

Wild rice, considered a whole grain, is really a long-grain marsh grass. Its distinctive, nutty flavor and chewy texture make it ideal for casseroles, soups and stews.

1 Serving: Calories 320 (Calories from Fat 80); Total Fat 9g (Saturated Fat 3g; Trans Fat 0g); Cholesterol 40mg; Sodium 620mg; Total Carbohydrate 42g (Dietary Fiber 4g; Sugars 5g); Protein 19g **% Daily Value:** Vitamin A 20%; Vitamin C 35%; Calcium 8%; Iron 10% **Exchanges:** 1 Starch, 1½ Other Carbohydrate, 1 Vegetable, 2 Lean Meat, ½ Fat **Carbohydrate Choices:** 3

Meat Loaf

PREP TIME: **15 MINUTES** • START TO FINISH: **1 HOUR 25 MINUTES** • **6 SERVINGS** • WHOLE GRAIN SERVING: **½**

¾ cup old-fashioned oats

1 can (5.5 oz) vegetable juice

¾ lb extra-lean (at least 90%) ground beef

¾ lb lean ground turkey

2 tablespoons chopped fresh parsley

½ teaspoon Italian seasoning

½ teaspoon salt

¼ teaspoon pepper

1 small onion, chopped (¼ cup)

1 clove garlic, finely chopped

1 egg

¼ cup ketchup

1   Heat oven to 350°F. In small bowl, soak oats in vegetable juice 3 to 5 minutes.

2   In large bowl, mix oat mixture and remaining ingredients except ketchup. Press mixture evenly in ungreased 8 × 4- or 9 × 5-inch loaf pan. Spread ketchup over top of loaf.

3   Bake 1 hour to 1 hour 10 minutes or until meat thermometer inserted in center of loaf reads 160°F.

Betty Tip

Lean ground turkey and old-fashioned oats help cut fat and retain moistness in this tasty version of the all-family favorite.

1 Serving: Calories 210 (Calories from Fat 60); Total Fat 7g (Saturated Fat 2.5g; Trans Fat 0g); Cholesterol 110mg; Sodium 440mg; Total Carbohydrate 11g (Dietary Fiber 2g; Sugars 3g); Protein 27g **% Daily Value:** Vitamin A 15%; Vitamin C 10%; Calcium 4%; Iron 15% **Exchanges:** ½ Starch, 3 ½ Very Lean Meat, 1 Fat **Carbohydrate Choices:** 1

Apple-Rosemary Pork and Barley

PREP TIME: **30 MINUTES** • START TO FINISH: **1 HOUR 10 MINUTES** • **4 SERVINGS** • WHOLE GRAIN SERVING: **½**

2 cups apple juice

½ cup uncooked hulled barley

2 tablespoons chopped fresh or 2 teaspoons dried rosemary leaves, crushed

2 teaspoons canola oil

¾ lb pork tenderloin, cut into ½-inch slices

1 medium onion, chopped (½ cup)

1 clove garlic, finely chopped

¼ cup apple jelly

1 large unpeeled red cooking apple, sliced (1½ cups)

1 In 2-quart saucepan, heat apple juice to boiling. Stir in barley and 1 tablespoon of the rosemary; reduce heat to low. Cover; simmer 1 hour or until liquid is absorbed and barley is tender.

2 About 20 minutes before barley is done, in 10-inch nonstick skillet, heat oil over medium-high heat. Cook pork, onion, garlic and remaining 1 tablespoon rosemary in oil 6 to 8 minutes, stirring occasionally, until pork is no longer pink in center.

3 Stir apple jelly and apple slices into pork mixture. Cook 3 to 4 minutes, stirring occasionally, until apple is crisp-tender. Serve over barley.

Betty Tip

Experience the amazing flavor of toasted pecans or walnuts; sprinkle them on top of the pork and barley just before serving. (See page 17 for toasting directions.) Butternut, buttercup or acorn squash sprinkled with cinnamon and drizzled with honey would taste terrific with this fall-inspired dish.

1 Serving: Calories 370 (Calories from Fat 60); Total Fat 6g (Saturated Fat 1.5g; Trans Fat 0g); Cholesterol 55mg; Sodium 50mg; Total Carbohydrate 57g (Dietary Fiber 6g; Sugars 28g); Protein 22g **% Daily Value:** Vitamin A 0%; Vitamin C 6%; Calcium 4%; Iron 15% **Exchanges:** ½ Starch, 1 Fruit, 2½ Other Carbohydrate, 3 Very Lean Meat, ½ Fat **Carbohydrate Choices:** 4

Ginger Pork and Kasha

PREP TIME: **40 MINUTES** • START TO FINISH: **45 MINUTES** • **4 SERVINGS** • WHOLE GRAIN SERVING: **½**

⅓ cup teriyaki sauce

1 teaspoon grated gingerroot or ½ teaspoon ground ginger

1 clove garlic, finely chopped

¾ lb boneless pork loin, cut into thin strips

½ cup uncooked buckwheat kernels or groats (kasha)

1 egg white

1 cup boiling water

2 teaspoons canola oil

2 medium carrots, thinly sliced (1 cup)

1 medium green bell pepper, cut into 1-inch pieces

½ cup water

1 tablespoon cornstarch

1   In large bowl, mix teriyaki sauce, gingerroot and garlic. Stir in pork. Cover; refrigerate 20 to 30 minutes to marinate.

2   Meanwhile, in small bowl, mix kasha and egg white. In 8-inch skillet, cook kasha mixture over medium-high heat, stirring constantly, until kernels separate and dry. Transfer kasha to medium bowl. Pour 1 cup boiling water over kasha; let stand 10 to 15 minutes or until liquid is absorbed.

3   Remove pork from marinade; reserve marinade. In 10-inch nonstick skillet, heat oil over medium-high heat. Cook pork in oil about 5 minutes, stirring frequently, until no longer pink. Stir in carrots. Cover; cook 2 to 3 minutes or until carrots are crisp-tender. Stir in bell pepper. Cook 2 to 3 minutes, stirring frequently, until bell pepper is crisp-tender.

4   In small bowl, mix reserved marinade, ½ cup water and the cornstarch; stir into pork mixture. Heat to boiling. Boil 1 minute, stirring frequently. Stir in kasha; cook until thoroughly heated.

Betty Tip

Kasha, also known as buckwheat groats, is native to Russia and is one of the oldest grains. It has a hearty flavor that works well with ginger. Its small size makes it ideal in main dishes because it cooks quickly.

1 Serving: Calories 230 (Calories from Fat 50); Total Fat 6g (Saturated Fat 1.5g; Trans Fat 0g); Cholesterol 55mg; Sodium 1000mg; Total Carbohydrate 20g (Dietary Fiber 3g; Sugars 5g); Protein 24g **% Daily Value:** Vitamin A 80%; Vitamin C 20%; Calcium 2%; Iron 10% **Exchanges:** ½ Starch, ½ Other Carbohydrate, 1 Vegetable, 3 Very Lean Meat, 1 Fat **Carbohydrate Choices:** 1

Lemon Rice with Turkey

PREP TIME: **20 MINUTES** • START TO FINISH: **1 HOUR** • **6 SERVINGS** • WHOLE GRAIN SERVING: **1**

1 cup uncooked long-grain brown rice

2¾ cups water

8 medium green onions, chopped (½ cup)

2 cloves garlic, finely chopped

1 cup chicken broth

1½ lb uncooked turkey breast slices, about ¼ inch thick, cut into 3 × ¼ × ¼-inch strips

2 teaspoons grated lemon peel

⅓ cup lemon juice

1 tablespoon capers, rinsed, drained

¼ teaspoon pepper

3 tablespoons chopped fresh parsley

1 Cook brown rice in water as directed on package, or see page 16; drain if necessary.

2 In 12-inch skillet, cook onions, garlic and broth over medium heat about 3 minutes, stirring occasionally, until onions are tender.

3 Stir in turkey. Cook 3 minutes, stirring occasionally.

4 Stir in cooked rice and remaining ingredients except parsley. Cook about 3 minutes, stirring occasionally, until rice is hot and turkey is no longer pink in center. Remove from heat. Stir in parsley.

Betty Tip

To reduce fat, refrigerate the chicken broth before using; the fat will rise to the top and you can remove it easily.

1 Serving: Calories 240 (Calories from Fat 20); Total Fat 2.5g (Saturated Fat 0.5g; Trans Fat 0g); Cholesterol 75mg; Sodium 270mg; Total Carbohydrate 26g (Dietary Fiber 4g; Sugars 1g); Protein 30g **% Daily Value:** Vitamin A 6%; Vitamin C 8%; Calcium 4%; Iron 10% **Exchanges:** 1½ Starch, 3 ½ Very Lean Meat **Carbohydrate Choices:** 2

Cereal-Crusted Fish Fillets

PREP TIME: **30 MINUTES** • START TO FINISH: **30 MINUTES** • **4 SERVINGS** • WHOLE GRAIN SERVING: **1**

3 cups Wheaties® cereal

½ cup all-purpose flour

½ teaspoon salt

1 egg

¼ cup water

4 cod fillets (4 to 6 oz each)

2 tablespoons canola oil

1 Place cereal in resealable food-storage plastic bag or between sheets of waxed paper; crush with rolling pin. Place crushed cereal (about 1⅔ cups) in shallow dish. In another shallow dish, mix flour and salt. In third shallow dish, beat egg and water with fork.

2 Dip fish in flour, coating well; shake off excess. Dip floured fish in egg mixture, then in cereal, coating all sides completely. Place coated fish on ungreased cookie sheet.

3 In 12-inch nonstick skillet, heat oil over medium heat until hot. Keeping at least 1 inch between fish fillets and cooking in batches if needed, cook fish in oil 3 to 4 minutes on each side, turning once, until well browned and fish flakes easily with fork. If needed, place cooked fish on paper towels on cookie sheet and keep warm in 225°F oven while cooking remaining fish.

Betty Tip

Using whole-grain cereals as a breading or in baking is an easy way to work in whole grains, and because the cereal is fortified, it boosts vitamins and minerals in your favorite recipes. Pair these crispy fillets with Lemon-Parsley Three-Grain Pilaf (page 183), coleslaw and baby carrots.

1 Serving: Calories 340 (Calories from Fat 90); Total Fat 10g (Saturated Fat 1g; Trans Fat 0g); Cholesterol 115mg; Sodium 590mg; Total Carbohydrate 34g (Dietary Fiber 3g; Sugars 4g); Protein 28g **% Daily Value:** Vitamin A 10%; Vitamin C 6%; Calcium 4%; Iron 50% **Exchanges:** 2 Starch, 3 Very Lean Meat, 1½ Fat **Carbohydrate Choices:** 2

Spanish Rice Bake

PREP TIME: **20 MINUTES** • START TO FINISH: **1 HOUR 25 MINUTES** • **4 SERVINGS (1 CUP EACH)** •
WHOLE GRAIN SERVING: **1½**

2 tablespoons canola oil

1 cup uncooked long-grain brown rice

1 medium onion, chopped (½ cup)

1 small green bell pepper, chopped (½ cup)

1 cup frozen whole kernel corn (from 1-lb bag), thawed, drained

1 can (10¾ oz) condensed tomato soup

2½ cups boiling water

1 tablespoon chopped fresh cilantro, if desired

1 teaspoon chili powder

¼ teaspoon salt

1½ cups shredded reduced-fat Colby-Monterey Jack cheese blend (6 oz)

1   Heat oven to 375°F. Spray 2-quart casserole with cooking spray. In 10-inch skillet, heat oil over medium heat. Cook brown rice, onion and bell pepper in oil 6 to 8 minutes, stirring frequently, until rice is light brown and onion is tender. Stir in corn.

2   In casserole, mix remaining ingredients except cheese. Stir in rice mixture and 1 cup of the cheese.

3   Cover; bake 20 minutes. Stir mixture. Cover; bake about 30 minutes longer or until rice is tender. Stir mixture; sprinkle with remaining ½ cup cheese. Bake uncovered 2 to 3 minutes or until cheese is melted. Let stand 10 minutes before serving.

Betty Tip

This recipe serves 8 to 10 as a side dish, or it makes 4 main-dish servings. Meat lovers can stir in their favorite cooked meat with the rice mixture; use a 3-quart casserole. Cooked ground beef, diced pepperoni, crumbled cooked bacon or cooked sausage works well.

1 Serving: Calories 460 (Calories from Fat 160); Total Fat 18g (Saturated Fat 6g; Trans Fat 0g); Cholesterol 20mg; Sodium 960mg; Total Carbohydrate 59g (Dietary Fiber 8g; Sugars 9g); Protein 17g **% Daily Value:** Vitamin A 20%; Vitamin C 20%; Calcium 30%; Iron 10% **Exchanges:** 3 Starch, 1 Other Carbohydrate, 1 High-Fat Meat, 1½ Fat **Carbohydrate Choices:** 4

Sage and Garlic Vegetable Dinner

PREP TIME: **25 MINUTES** • START TO FINISH: **1 HOUR 20 MINUTES** • **5 SERVINGS (1 3/4 CUPS EACH)** •
WHOLE GRAIN SERVING: ½

1¾ cups water

½ cup uncooked hulled barley

1 medium butternut squash, peeled, cut into 1-inch pieces (3 cups)

2 medium parsnips, peeled, cut into 1-inch slices, then cut large slices in half crosswise (about 1 cup)

1 medium onion, coarsely chopped (½ cup)

2 cloves garlic, finely chopped

2 cups frozen cut green beans, thawed

2 cans (14 oz each) stewed tomatoes, undrained

½ cup water

1 teaspoon dried sage leaves

½ teaspoon seasoned salt

1   In 5-quart Dutch oven, heat water to boiling over high heat. Stir in barley; reduce heat to low. Cover; simmer 40 minutes.

2   Stir in remaining ingredients; return to boiling over medium-high heat. Reduce heat to low; cover and simmer 30 minutes longer or until vegetables and barley are tender.

Betty Tip

Butternut squash is peanut shaped and has a peel that ranges from cream to yellow. Inside, the squash is bright orange and sweet.

1 Serving: Calories 200 (Calories from Fat 5); Total Fat 0.5g (Saturated Fat 0g; Trans Fat 0g); Cholesterol 0mg; Sodium 610mg; Total Carbohydrate 44g (Dietary Fiber 8g; Sugars 15g); Protein 5g **% Daily Value:** Vitamin A 170%; Vitamin C 25%; Calcium 10%; Iron 15% **Exchanges:** 1 Starch, 1 Other Carbohydrate, 2 Vegetable **Carbohydrate Choices:** 3

Easy-Does-It Barley Paella

PREP TIME: **30 MINUTES** • START TO FINISH: **1 HOUR 30 MINUTES** • **5 SERVINGS (1 1/2 CUPS EACH)** •
WHOLE GRAIN SERVING: **1**

2 cups reduced-sodium chicken broth

½ cup uncooked hulled barley

4 oz bulk chorizo sausage

1 medium onion, chopped (½ cup)

1 small red bell pepper, chopped (½ cup)

3 cloves garlic, finely chopped

1 can (14.5 oz) petite diced tomatoes, undrained

1 teaspoon smoked Spanish paprika

1½ cups 1-inch pieces cooked chicken breast

4 oz frozen cooked cocktail shrimp (from 12-oz bag), thawed, drained and tail shells removed

1 cup frozen sweet peas, thawed

1 can (14 oz) artichoke hearts, drained, cut into fourths

1   In 5-quart Dutch oven, heat broth to boiling. Stir in barley. Reduce heat to low; cover and simmer 1 hour or until tender.

2   Fifteen minutes before barley is done, heat 10-inch nonstick skillet over high heat. Add sausage; cook 2 minutes, stirring occasionally, to crumble. Reduce heat to medium-high. Add onion, bell pepper and garlic; cook 4 to 5 minutes, stirring occasionally, until onion is slightly browned. Set aside.

3   Stir tomatoes and paprika into barley. Return to boiling. Stir in cooked onion mixture and remaining ingredients. Cook, stirring constantly, 3 to 4 minutes or until thoroughly heated.

Betty Tip

This recipe received rave reviews at our taste panels and will in your home, too. If you have trouble finding smoked Spanish paprika, substitute 1 teaspoon sweet paprika and ¼ teaspoon liquid smoke.

1 Serving: Calories 360 (Calories from Fat 100); Total Fat 11g (Saturated Fat 4g; Trans Fat 0g); Cholesterol 100mg; Sodium 910mg; Total Carbohydrate 34g (Dietary Fiber 9g; Sugars 6g); Protein 31g
% Daily Value: Vitamin A 30%; Vitamin C 40%; Calcium 10%; Iron 25% **Exchanges:** 1 Starch, 1 Other Carbohydrate, 1 Vegetable, 3½ Lean Meat **Carbohydrate Choices:** 2

Toasted Barley with Mixed Vegetables

PREP TIME: **30 MINUTES** • START TO FINISH: **1 HOUR 10 MINUTES** • **6 SERVINGS (1 CUP EACH)** •
WHOLE GRAIN SERVING: ½

½ cup uncooked hulled barley

1 can (14 oz) chicken broth

2 large onions, chopped
(2 cups)

2 packages (8 oz each) sliced
mushrooms (6 cups)

4 medium carrots, cut into
julienne (matchstick) strips
(2 cups)

1 large red bell pepper,
coarsely chopped (1 cup)

2 tablespoons chopped fresh
or 1 tablespoon dried dill
weed

½ teaspoon pepper

4 medium green onions,
chopped (1/4 cup)

1 Spray 12-inch skillet with cooking spray. Cook barley in skillet over medium heat 6 to 8 minutes, stirring frequently until barley begins to brown, then stirring constantly until golden brown. Reduce heat to low; add broth. Cover; simmer 40 minutes.

2 Stir in remaining ingredients except green onions. Heat to boiling over high heat. Reduce heat to low; cover and simmer 20 minutes or until vegetables are tender. Sprinkle with green onions.

Betty Tip

Barley was one of the first grains ever cultivated and contains many nutrients. One cup of cooked barley provides the same amount of protein as a glass of milk. It also contains niacin, thiamin and potassium.

1 Serving: Calories 140 (Calories from Fat 10); Total Fat 1g (Saturated Fat 0g; Trans Fat 0g); Cholesterol 0mg; Sodium 320mg; Total Carbohydrate 26g (Dietary Fiber 6g; Sugars 6g); Protein 6g **% Daily Value:** Vitamin A 100%; Vitamin C 25%; Calcium 4%; Iron 8% **Exchanges:** 1 Starch, ½ Other Carbohydrate, 1 Vegetable **Carbohydrate Choices:** 2

Canadian Bacon–Whole Wheat Pizza

PREP TIME: **15 MINUTES** • START TO FINISH: **55 MINUTES** • **8 SERVINGS** • WHOLE GRAIN SERVING: **2**

1 package regular active or fast-acting dry yeast

1 cup warm water (105°F to 115°F)

2½ cups whole wheat flour

2 tablespoons olive oil

½ teaspoon salt

1 tablespoon olive oil

1 tablespoon whole-grain cornmeal

1 can (8 oz) pizza sauce

2 cups finely shredded Italian mozzarella and Parmesan cheese blend (8 oz)

1 package (6 oz) sliced Canadian bacon, cut into fourths

1 small green bell pepper, chopped (½ cup)

1 In medium bowl, dissolve yeast in warm water. Stir in flour, 2 tablespoons oil and the salt. Beat vigorously with spoon 20 strokes. Let dough rest 20 minutes.

2 Move oven rack to lowest position. Heat oven to 425°F. Grease cookie sheet with 1 tablespoon oil; sprinkle with cornmeal. Pat dough into 12 × 10-inch rectangle on cookie sheet, using floured fingers; pinch edges to form ½-inch rim.

3 Spread pizza sauce over crust. Top with cheese, bacon and bell pepper. Bake 15 to 20 minutes or until edge of crust is golden brown.

Betty Tip

All whole wheat pizza crust makes a great base for the family-friendly Canadian bacon and cheese toppings. Vary the flavor by using different toppings, such as pepperoni, cooked and drained ground beef, vegetables and different types of cheese.

1 Serving: Calories 320 (Calories from Fat 130); Total Fat 14g (Saturated Fat 6g; Trans Fat 0g); Cholesterol 35mg; Sodium 750mg; Total Carbohydrate 32g (Dietary Fiber 5g; Sugars 3g); Protein 16g **% Daily Value:** Vitamin A 6%; Vitamin C 8%; Calcium 20%; Iron 15% **Exchanges:** 1 Starch, 1 Other Carbohydrate, 2 Medium-Fat Meat, ½ Fat **Carbohydrate Choices:** 2

Beef and Millet Stew in Bread Bowls

PREP TIME: **20 MINUTES** • START TO FINISH: **1 HOUR 30 MINUTES** • **6 SERVINGS** (1 BOWL AND 1¼ CUPS STEW EACH) •
WHOLE GRAIN SERVING: ½

Bread Bowls

1 loaf (about 1 lb) frozen 100% whole wheat bread dough, thawed

1 tablespoon olive oil

1 teaspoon dried basil leaves

Stew

2 teaspoons olive oil

1 lb lean beef stew meat, cut into small pieces

1 medium onion, chopped (½ cup)

2 cloves garlic, finely chopped

2 teaspoons herbes de Provence *

½ teaspoon salt

¼ teaspoon pepper

1 can (14 oz) reduced-sodium beef broth

1 can (28 oz) diced tomatoes, undrained

½ cup water

½ cup uncooked millet

1 cup ready-to-eat baby-cut carrots, cut in half lengthwise

1 cup frozen cut green beans

* 1 teaspoon dried basil leaves plus 1 teaspoon dried rosemary leaves can be substituted for the herbes de Provence.

1 Lightly grease outsides of 6 (10-ounce) custard cups with shortening. (Do not use cooking spray.) Place cups upside down on large cookie sheet.

2 Divide dough into 6 equal pieces. Shape each piece into ball. Roll or pat each ball into 6-inch round. Place dough round over bottom of each custard cup, stretching to fit. Brush dough with 1 tablespoon oil; sprinkle with basil. Cover; let rise in warm place 20 minutes.

3 Heat oven to 350°F. Bake bread bowls 16 to 20 minutes or until golden brown. Cool 5 minutes; remove from cups to cooling rack. Cool completely, about 30 minutes. (Interiors of bread bowls may be slightly moist.)

4 Meanwhile, in 3-quart saucepan, heat 2 teaspoons oil over medium-high heat. Add beef, onion, garlic, herbes de Provence, salt and pepper. Cook 5 to 6 minutes, stirring occasionally, until beef is lightly browned.

5 Stir in broth, tomatoes and water. Heat to boiling. Reduce heat to low. Cover; simmer 45 minutes. Stir in millet, carrots and green beans. Cook uncovered about 25 minutes or until beef is tender. Serve stew in bread bowls.

Betty Tip

These individual bread bowls with millet stew are adorable. Millet is high in protein, B vitamins, copper and iron. An added benefit is that millet does not contain gluten, so it can be tolerated by anyone allergic to wheat.

1 Serving: Calories 490 (Calories from Fat 160); Total Fat 17g (Saturated Fat 5g; Trans Fat 1g); Cholesterol 45mg; Sodium 870mg; Total Carbohydrate 58g (Dietary Fiber 9g; Sugars 13g); Protein 26g
% Daily Value: Vitamin A 50%; Vitamin C 15%; Calcium 15%; Iron 40% **Exchanges:** 2½ Starch, 1 Other Carbohydrate, 1 Vegetable, 2½ Medium-Fat Meat, ½ Fat **Carbohydrate Choices:** 4

slow cooker sides and meals

6

Rye Berries with Butternut Squash
Page 164

Savory Slow-Cooked Grains

PREP TIME: **25 MINUTES** • START TO FINISH: **6 HOURS 55 MINUTES** • **6 MAIN-DISH SERVINGS** (1⅓ CUPS EACH)
OR 16 SIDE-DISH SERVINGS (½ CUP EACH) • WHOLE GRAIN SERVING: 1½

1 cup uncooked long-grain brown rice

½ cup uncooked wild rice

½ cup uncooked green lentils

3 cups coarsely chopped fresh mushrooms (8 oz)

2 medium carrots, coarsely chopped (1 cup)

12 medium green onions, chopped (¾ cup)

1 container (32 oz) roasted vegetable stock or chicken broth (4 cups)

1 cup water

2 tablespoons reduced-sodium soy sauce

2 tablespoons dry sherry, if desired

2 tablespoons butter or margarine, melted

½ teaspoon dried thyme leaves

½ teaspoon garlic salt

¼ cup chopped walnuts, toasted (page 17)

⅓ cup finely chopped parsley

1   In 3- to 4-quart slow cooker, mix all ingredients except walnuts and parsley.

2   Cover; cook on Low heat setting 6 hours 30 minutes to 7 hours 30 minutes.

3   Stir before serving. Sprinkle with walnuts and parsley.

Betty Tip

This is a great starter recipe if you're new to whole grains. Using a slow cooker is a terrific way to prepare them because some grains take a while to cook.

1 Serving: Calories 330 (Calories from Fat 80); Total Fat 9g (Saturated Fat 3g; Trans Fat 0g); Cholesterol 10mg; Sodium 980mg; Total Carbohydrate 51g (Dietary Fiber 9g; Sugars 5g); Protein 12g **% Daily Value:** Vitamin A 80%; Vitamin C 8%; Calcium 6%; Iron 20% **Exchanges:** 2 Starch, 1 Other Carbohydrate, 1 Vegetable, ½ Very Lean Meat, 1½ Fat **Carbohydrate Choices:** 3 ½

Three-Grain Medley

PREP TIME: **10 MINUTES** • START TO FINISH: **4 HOURS 10 MINUTES** • **4 MAIN-DISH SERVINGS** •
WHOLE GRAIN SERVING: **1½**

⅔ cup uncooked wheat berries

½ cup uncooked hulled or pearl
barley

½ cup uncooked wild rice

¼ cup chopped fresh parsley

¼ cup butter, melted, or canola
oil

2 teaspoons finely shredded
lemon peel

6 medium green onions, thinly
sliced (6 tablespoons)

2 cloves garlic, finely chopped

2 cans (14 oz each) vegetable
or chicken broth

1 jar (2 oz) diced pimientos,
undrained

1   In 3- to 4-quart slow cooker, mix all ingredients.

2   Cover; cook on Low heat setting 4 to 6 hours or until liquid is
absorbed. Stir before serving.

Betty Tip

Use this scrumptious grain filling to stuff bell peppers. Steam-cleaned
bell pepper halves (any color that you are in the mood for) just until
tender so that they still hold their shape. Spoon the hot cooked grain
mixture into the halves, and sprinkle with shredded Parmesan cheese.

1 Serving: Calories 370 (Calories from Fat 110); Total Fat 13g (Saturated Fat 8g; Trans Fat 0.5g);
Cholesterol 30mg; Sodium 970mg; Total Carbohydrate 56g (Dietary Fiber 8g; Sugars 5g); Protein 9g
% Daily Value: Vitamin A 45%; Vitamin C 20%; Calcium 4%; Iron 15%   **Exchanges:** 3 Starch, ½ Other
Carbohydrate, 2 Fat   **Carbohydrate Choices:** 4

Turkey–Wild Rice Casserole

PREP TIME: **25 MINUTES** • START TO FINISH: **5 HOURS 25 MINUTES** • **5 MAIN-DISH SERVINGS** •
WHOLE GRAIN SERVING: **1½**

4 slices bacon, cut into ½-inch pieces

1 lb turkey breast tenderloins, cut into ½- to 1-inch pieces

2 medium carrots, coarsely chopped (1 cup)

1 medium onion, coarsely chopped (½ cup)

1 medium stalk celery, sliced (½ cup)

1 cup uncooked wild rice

1 can (10¾ oz) condensed cream of chicken soup

2½ cups water

2 tablespoons reduced-sodium soy sauce

¼ to ½ teaspoon dried marjoram leaves

⅛ teaspoon pepper

1   In 12-inch skillet, cook bacon over medium heat, stirring occasionally, until almost crisp. Stir in turkey, carrots, onion and celery. Cook about 2 minutes, stirring frequently, until turkey is brown.

2   Spoon turkey mixture into 3- to 4-quart slow cooker. Stir in remaining ingredients.

3   Cover; cook on Low heat setting 5 to 6 hours.

Betty Tip

Wild rice is native to the Great Lakes, but also grown in the Midwest and California. Wild rice has a wonderful nutty flavor and chewy texture that enhances casseroles, soups, stuffings and salads.

1 Serving: Calories 340 (Calories from Fat 70); Total Fat 8g (Saturated Fat 2.5g; Trans Fat 0g); Cholesterol 70mg; Sodium 870mg; Total Carbohydrate 38g (Dietary Fiber 4g; Sugars 3g); Protein 30g **% Daily Value:** Vitamin A 70%; Vitamin C 2%; Calcium 4%; Iron 15% **Exchanges:** 2½ Starch, 3 Very Lean Meat, 1 Fat **Carbohydrate Choices:** 2½

Barley and Pine Nut Casserole

PREP TIME: **15 MINUTES** • START TO FINISH: **6 HOURS 15 MINUTES** • **6 SIDE-DISH SERVINGS** (¾ CUP EACH) •
WHOLE GRAIN SERVING: **1**

1 cup uncooked hulled or lightly
   pearled barley

1½ cups vegetable juice

½ teaspoon salt

¼ teaspoon pepper

2 medium stalks celery, sliced
   (1 cup)

1 medium bell pepper, chopped
   (1 cup)

1 medium onion, chopped
   (½ cup)

1 can (14 oz) vegetable or
   chicken broth

4 medium green onions, sliced
   (¼ cup)

¼ cup pine nuts, toasted
   (page 17)

1 In 3- to 4-quart slow cooker, mix all ingredients except green onions and nuts.

2 Cover; cook on Low heat setting 6 to 8 hours.

3 Stir in green onions and nuts.

Betty Tip

Though pearled barley is a common form of barley, the bran has been removed, so it's not a whole grain. Hulled barley is whole grain, but may be harder to find—look for it in a food co-op or buy it online.

1 Serving: Calories 190 (Calories from Fat 35); Total Fat 4g (Saturated Fat 0.5g; Trans Fat 0g); Cholesterol 0mg; Sodium 660mg; Total Carbohydrate 34g (Dietary Fiber 7g; Sugars 5g); Protein 5g **% Daily Value:** Vitamin A 30%; Vitamin C 35%; Calcium 4%; Iron 8% **Exchanges:** 1 Starch, 1 Other Carbohydrate, 1 Vegetable, ½ Fat **Carbohydrate Choices:** 2

Bulgur Pilaf with Broccoli and Carrots

PREP TIME: **20 MINUTES** • START TO FINISH: **6 HOURS 35 MINUTES** • **8 MAIN-DISH SERVINGS** •
WHOLE GRAIN SERVING: **1½**

2 cups uncooked bulgur wheat
    or cracked wheat

1 tablespoon butter or
    margarine, melted

1 teaspoon salt

4 medium carrots, shredded
    (2⅔ cups)

1 large onion, chopped (1 cup)

2 cans (14 oz each) vegetable
    or chicken broth

4 cups chopped fresh broccoli

1 cup shredded Colby cheese
    (4 oz)

1   In 4- to 5-quart slow cooker, mix all ingredients except broccoli and cheese.

2   Cover; cook on Low heat setting 6 to 8 hours or just until bulgur is tender.

3   Stir in broccoli. Sprinkle with cheese. Increase heat setting to High. Cover; cook about 15 minutes or until broccoli is tender and cheese is melted.

Betty Tip

A nice change of pace from the more common rice pilaf, this meatless bulgur entrée is sure to satisfy both young and old. Serve it with a citrus fruit salad of orange and grapefruit sections drizzled with a poppy seed fruit dressing or your favorite fruit dressing.

1 Serving: Calories 250 (Calories from Fat 60); Total Fat 7g (Saturated Fat 4g; Trans Fat 0g); Cholesterol 20mg; Sodium 860mg; Total Carbohydrate 37g (Dietary Fiber 9g; Sugars 5g); Protein 10g **% Daily Value:** Vitamin A 110%; Vitamin C 35%; Calcium 15%; Iron 8% **Exchanges:** 1½ Starch, ½ Other Carbohydrate, 1 Vegetable, ½ High-Fat Meat, ½ Fat **Carbohydrate Choices:** 2½

Mediterranean Bulgur and Lentils

PREP TIME: **15 MINUTES** • START TO FINISH: **3 HOURS 30 MINUTES** • **8 MAIN-DISH SERVINGS** • WHOLE GRAIN SERVING: **½**

1 cup uncooked bulgur wheat or cracked wheat

½ cup dried lentils, sorted, rinsed

1 teaspoon ground cumin

¼ teaspoon salt

3 cloves garlic, finely chopped

1 can (15.25 oz) whole kernel corn, drained

2 cans (14 oz each) vegetable or chicken broth

2 medium tomatoes, chopped (1½ cups)

½ cup drained pitted kalamata olives

1 cup crumbled reduced-fat Feta cheese (4 oz)

1   In 3- to 4-quart slow cooker, mix all ingredients except tomatoes, olives and cheese.

2   Cover; cook on low heat setting 3 to 4 hours or until lentils are tender.

3   Stir in tomatoes and olives. Increase heat setting to high. Cover; cook 15 minutes longer. Top with cheese.

Betty Tip

You have a little of everything in this dish: grains, vegetables and cheese. Use warmed pita bread wedges to scoop up every delicious bite. A green salad with a drizzle of olive oil and a spritz of lemon juice is a nice addition.

1 Serving: Calories 210 (Calories from Fat 35); Total Fat 4g (Saturated Fat 1.5g; Trans Fat 0g); Cholesterol 0mg; Sodium 880mg; Total Carbohydrate 33g (Dietary Fiber 7g; Sugars 4g); Protein 10g **% Daily Value:** Vitamin A 20%; Vitamin C 8%; Calcium 8%; Iron 15% **Exchanges:** 2 Starch, ½ Very Lean Meat, ½ Fat **Carbohydrate Choices:** 2

Wild Rice with Cranberries

PREP TIME: **15 MINUTES** • START TO FINISH: **4 HOURS 30 MINUTES** • **8 SIDE-DISH SERVINGS** • WHOLE GRAIN SERVING: **1½**

1½ cups uncooked wild rice

1 tablespoon butter or
    margarine, melted

½ teaspoon salt

¼ teaspoon pepper

4 medium green onions, sliced
    (¼ cup)

2 cans (14 oz each) vegetable
    or chicken broth

1 can (4 oz) sliced mushrooms,
    undrained

½ cup slivered almonds,
    toasted (page 17)

1/3 cup sweetened dried
    cranberries

1   In 3- to 4-quart slow cooker, mix all ingredients except almonds and cranberries.

2   Cover; cook on Low heat setting 4 to 5 hours or until wild rice is tender.

3   Stir in almonds and cranberries. Cover; cook on Low heat setting 15 minutes longer.

Betty Tip

Toasting the almonds not only enhances their flavor and color but also helps prevent them from becoming soggy after they are stirred into the wild rice mixture. The nuttiness and chewiness of nuts and grains complement each other.

1 Serving: Calories 210 (Calories from Fat 50); Total Fat 5g (Saturated Fat 1.5g; Trans Fat 0g); Cholesterol 0mg; Sodium 640mg; Total Carbohydrate 33g (Dietary Fiber 4g; Sugars 6g); Protein 7g
% Daily Value: Vitamin A 10%; Vitamin C 0%; Calcium 2%; Iron 8% **Exchanges:** 2 Starch, 1 Fat
Carbohydrate Choices: 2

Chicken-Barley Stew

PREP TIME: **15 MINUTES** • START TO FINISH: **8 HOURS 30 MINUTES** • **6 MAIN-DISH SERVINGS** (1½ CUPS EACH) •
WHOLE GRAIN SERVING: ½

3 large carrots, sliced (2 cups)

2 medium stalks celery, sliced (1 cup)

1 large onion, chopped (1 cup)

2 bone-in chicken breasts (about 1¼ lb), skin removed

5 cups water

¾ cup uncooked hulled or pearl barley

2 teaspoons chicken bouillon granules

1 teaspoon salt

¼ teaspoon pepper

1 can (14.5 oz) diced tomatoes, undrained

2 tablespoons chopped fresh parsley

1 teaspoon dried thyme leaves

1   In 4- to 5-quart slow cooker, place carrots, celery and onion. Place chicken breasts on vegetables. Add remaining ingredients except parsley and thyme.

2   Cover; cook on Low heat setting 8 to 9 hours.

3   Remove chicken from cooker; place on cutting board. Remove meat from bones and chop into ½- to 1-inch pieces; discard bones.

4   Stir chicken, parsley and thyme into stew. Increase heat setting to High. Cover; cook 10 to 15 minutes longer or until chicken is thoroughly heated.

Betty Tip

For the can of diced tomatoes, try a variety seasoned with Italian herbs or roasted garlic for an additional boost of flavor. This hearty stew pairs beautifully with any mixed greens and crusty whole-grain rolls.

1 Serving: Calories 220 (Calories from Fat 25); Total Fat 3g (Saturated Fat 0.5g; Trans Fat 0g); Cholesterol 40mg; Sodium 850mg; Total Carbohydrate 30g (Dietary Fiber 7g; Sugars 6g); Protein 19g
% Daily Value: Vitamin A 100%; Vitamin C 10%; Calcium 8%; Iron 15% **Exchanges:** 1 Starch, ½ Other Carbohydrate, 2 Vegetable, 2 Very Lean Meat **Carbohydrate Choices:** 2

Ham and Wild Rice Soup

PREP TIME: **10 MINUTES** • START TO FINISH: **8 HOURS 25 MINUTES** • **8 SERVINGS** (1 CUP EACH) • WHOLE GRAIN SERVING: **½**

2 cups diced cooked ham

¾ cup uncooked wild rice

1 medium onion, chopped
    (½ cup)

1 bag (1 lb) frozen mixed
    vegetables, thawed,
    drained

1 can (14 oz) chicken broth

1 can (10¾ oz) cream of celery
    soup

¼ teaspoon pepper

3 cups water

½ cup half-and-half

1   In 3- to 4-quart slow cooker, mix all ingredients except half-and-half.

2   Cover; cook on Low heat setting 8 to 9 hours.

3   Stir in half-and-half. Increase heat setting to High. Cover; cook 10 to 15 minutes longer or until hot.

Betty Tip

Cooking wild rice on the stove-top can take up to 50 minutes, so using a slow cooker is an easy alternative. To quickly thaw frozen vegetables, rinse them under cold, running water. It's best to thaw frozen veggies before adding them to a slow cooker recipe.

1 Serving: Calories 210 (Calories from Fat 60); Total Fat 6g (Saturated Fat 2.5g; Trans Fat 0g); Cholesterol 25mg; Sodium 920mg; Total Carbohydrate 25g (Dietary Fiber 4g; Sugars 5g); Protein 13g **% Daily Value:** Vitamin A 50%; Vitamin C 2%; Calcium 6%; Iron 10% **Exchanges:** 1½ Starch, 1 Vegetable, 1 Lean Meat, ½ Fat **Carbohydrate Choices:** 1½

Chicken, Sausage and Cabbage Stew

PREP TIME: **20 MINUTES** • START TO FINISH: **6 HOURS 20 MINUTES** • **8 SERVINGS** • WHOLE GRAIN SERVING: **1**

2 cups coarsely chopped
(1-inch pieces) cabbage

1 cup ready-to-eat baby-cut
carrots, cut lengthwise into
quarters

1 cup uncooked wild rice

1 medium onion, chopped
(½ cup)

2 cloves garlic, finely chopped

1 package (8 oz) sliced
mushrooms (3 cups)

1 lb boneless skinless chicken
thighs, cut into 1½-inch
pieces

½ lb sweet Italian sausage links
(about 2), cut into 1-inch
pieces

2 cans (14 oz each) chicken
broth

1 can (10¾ oz) condensed
cream of mushroom soup

1 In 4- to 5-quart slow cooker, mix all ingredients except broth and soup.

2 In medium bowl, mix broth and soup. Pour over meat and vegetables in slow cooker; stir gently until blended.

3 Cover; cook on Low heat setting 6 to 8 hours.

Betty Tip

Some foods are actually better the next day, and this recipe is one of them. Store leftover stew in a resealable plastic food-storage bag or plastic bowl with a tight-fitting lid, and refrigerate for up to 2 days. To reheat, place stew in a microwavable dish and cover loosely. Microwave on High 1 to 2 minutes or until hot.

1 Serving: Calories 310 (Calories from Fat 120); Total Fat 13g (Saturated Fat 4g; Trans Fat 0g); Cholesterol 55mg; Sodium 830mg; Total Carbohydrate 25g (Dietary Fiber 3g; Sugars 4g); Protein 24g **% Daily Value:** Vitamin A 40%; Vitamin C 8%; Calcium 6%; Iron 15% **Exchanges:** 1 Starch, ½ Other Carbohydrate, 1 Vegetable, 2½ Lean Meat, 1 Fat **Carbohydrate Choices:** 1½

Vegetable-Beef-Barley Soup

PREP TIME: **20 MINUTES** • START TO FINISH: **8 HOURS 20 MINUTES** • **10 SERVINGS** (1⅓ CUPS EACH) • WHOLE GRAIN SERVING: ½

¾ cup frozen cut green beans

⅔ cup frozen whole kernel corn

1½ lb beef stew meat

½ cup chopped bell pepper

1 large onion, chopped (1 cup)

⅔ cup uncooked hulled or pearl barley

1½ cups water

1 teaspoon salt

1 teaspoon chopped fresh or ½ teaspoon dried thyme leaves

¼ teaspoon pepper

2 cans (14 oz each) beef broth

2 cans (14.5 oz each) diced tomatoes with roasted garlic, undrained

1 can (8 oz) tomato sauce

1 Spray 5- to 6-quart slow cooker with cooking spray. Rinse green beans and corn with cold water to separate and partially thaw. Mix green beans, corn and remaining ingredients in cooker.

2 Cover; cook on Low heat setting 8 to 9 hours.

Betty Tip

Select lean stew meat, and trim any extra fat before adding it to the soup. Top this soup with a handful of herb-flavored croutons and a little shredded Parmesan cheese.

1 Serving: Calories 220 (Calories from Fat 80); Total Fat 9g (Saturated Fat 3g; Trans Fat 0g); Cholesterol 40mg; Sodium 840mg; Total Carbohydrate 20g (Dietary Fiber 4g; Sugars 5g); Protein 16g **% Daily Value:** Vitamin A 6%; Vitamin C 15%; Calcium 6%; Iron 20% **Exchanges:** 1 Starch, 1 Vegetable, 1½ Medium-Fat Meat **Carbohydrate Choices:** 1

Lentil Stew with Cornbread Dumplings

PREP TIME: **15 MINUTES** • START TO FINISH: **7 HOURS 50 MINUTES** • **8 SERVINGS** (ABOUT 1 CUP STEW AND 1 DUMPLING EACH) •
WHOLE GRAIN SERVING: ½

Stew

1 lb dried lentils (2 cups),
   sorted, rinsed

3 cups water

1 teaspoon ground cumin

1 teaspoon salt-free seasoning
   blend

3 medium carrots, thinly sliced
   (1½ cups)

1 medium yellow or red bell
   pepper, cut into 1-inch
   pieces

1 medium onion, chopped
   (½ cup)

1 can (14.5 oz) diced tomatoes
   with green chiles,
   undrained

1 can (14 oz) vegetable or
   chicken broth

Dumplings

½ cup all-purpose flour

½ cup whole-grain yellow
   cornmeal

1 teaspoon baking powder

¼ teaspoon salt

¼ cup milk

2 tablespoons canola oil

1 egg, slightly beaten

1 In 3- to 4-quart slow cooker, mix all stew ingredients.

2 Cover; cook on Low heat setting 7 to 8 hours.

3 In medium bowl, mix flour, cornmeal, baking powder and salt.
Stir in milk, oil and egg just until moistened. Drop dough by spoonfuls
onto hot lentil mixture. Increase heat setting to High. Cover; cook
25 to 35 minutes or until toothpick inserted in center of dumplings
comes out clean.

Betty Tip

The lentils, vegetables and cornmeal create a main dish
that is high in fiber. To get the most whole-grain benefit,
look for a package label that says whole-grain cornmeal.

1 Serving: Calories 330 (Calories from Fat 45); Total Fat 5g (Saturated Fat 0.5g; Trans Fat 0g);
Cholesterol 25mg; Sodium 530mg; Total Carbohydrate 52g (Dietary Fiber 12g; Sugars 6g); Protein 18g
% Daily Value: Vitamin A 70%; Vitamin C 30%; Calcium 10%; Iron 35% **Exchanges:** 3½ Starch,
1 Very Lean Meat, ½ Fat **Carbohydrate Choices:** 3½

Black-Eyed Pea and Sausage Soup

PREP TIME: **15 MINUTES** • START TO FINISH: **8 HOURS 30 MINUTES** • **6 SERVINGS** • WHOLE GRAIN SERVING: ½

2 cans (15 to 16 oz each) black-eyed peas, drained, rinsed

12 oz smoked turkey kielbasa sausage, cut lengthwise in half, then sliced crosswise

4 medium carrots, chopped (2 cups)

4 cloves garlic, finely chopped

1 cup uncooked wheat berries

2 cups water

3 cans (14 oz each) reduced-sodium beef broth

2 cups shredded fresh spinach

1 teaspoon dried marjoram leaves

1 In 3- to 4-quart slow cooker, mix all ingredients except spinach and marjoram.

2 Cover; cook on Low heat setting 8 to 9 hours.

3 Stir in spinach and marjoram. Cover; cook on Low heat setting about 15 minutes longer or until spinach is tender.

Betty Tip

Offer diners Dijon mustard and horseradish to stir into this Southern-style soup. Try other greens, like Swiss chard, mustard greens or turnip greens, solo or in combination with the spinach. You might also try andouille sausage, a Cajun favorite, to give this soup a kick.

1 Serving: Calories 350 (Calories from Fat 70); Total Fat 8g (Saturated Fat 2g; Trans Fat 0g); Cholesterol 30mg; Sodium 950mg; Total Carbohydrate 47g (Dietary Fiber 9g; Sugars 3g); Protein 25g
% Daily Value: Vitamin A 120%; Vitamin C 6%; Calcium 8%; Iron 25% **Exchanges:** 3 Starch, 2 Lean Meat **Carbohydrate Choices:** 3

Cinnamon Overnight Oatmeal

PREP TIME: **10 MINUTES** • START TO FINISH: **7 HOURS 10 MINUTES** • **4 SERVINGS** (¾ CUP EACH) • WHOLE GRAIN SERVING: **1**

1 cup steel-cut oats

¼ cup packed brown sugar

⅛ teaspoon salt

3¼ cups water

½ cup half-and-half

½ cup diced dried fruits and raisins (from 7-oz bag)

1 teaspoon ground cinnamon

⅓ cup chopped walnuts, if desired

1   Spray 3- to 4-quart slow cooker with cooking spray. Place oats, brown sugar and salt in slow cooker. Cover with water and half-and-half. Stir to mix slightly.

2   Cover; cook on Low heat setting 7 to 8 hours.

3   Stir in dried fruits and cinnamon. Top with walnuts.

Betty Tip

Steel-cut oats, also known as Scottish or Irish oats, are kernels of the oat sliced lengthwise. They require a longer cooking time, typically 20 minutes on the stove-top. Starting the oatmeal in the slow cooker the night before allows you to have a scrumptious breakfast ready and waiting for you in the morning.

1 Serving: Calories 220 (Calories from Fat 45); Total Fat 5g (Saturated Fat 2.5g; Trans Fat 0g); Cholesterol 10mg; Sodium 100mg; Total Carbohydrate 40g (Dietary Fiber 4g; Sugars 23g); Protein 5g **% Daily Value:** Vitamin A 6%; Vitamin C 0%; Calcium 8%; Iron 8% **Exchanges:** 1 Starch, 1½ Other Carbohydrate, 1 Fat **Carbohydrate Choices:** 2½

Orange-Cranberry Rye and Barley Pilaf

PREP TIME: **15 MINUTES** • START TO FINISH: **8 HOURS 15 MINUTES** • **8 SIDE-DISH SERVINGS** (½ CUP EACH) •
WHOLE GRAIN SERVING: ½

1 cup uncooked rye berries

½ cup uncooked hulled barley

2 medium stalks celery, sliced (1 cup)

⅓ cup finely chopped onion

2 small parsnips or carrots, peeled, sliced (1½ cups)

½ teaspoon salt

1 can (14 oz) chicken broth

1¼ cups water

⅓ cup sweetened dried cranberries

1 teaspoon grated orange peel

1   Spray 3- to 4-quart slow cooker with cooking spray. Place all ingredients except cranberries and orange peel in slow cooker.

2   Cover; cook on Low heat setting 8 to 9 hours or until rye berries are chewy but tender.

3   Stir in cranberries and orange peel just before serving.

Betty Tip

Rye berries and hulled barley can usually be found in co-ops or natural-food stores or through the Internet. They take a long time to cook, making them ideal to prepare in the slow cooker. The texture of rye berries is similar to wheat berries, only slightly more chewy. If you love grains, this chewy, flavorful side dish will soon become a new favorite.

1 Serving: Calories 260 (Calories from Fat 15); Total Fat 1.5g (Saturated Fat 0g; Trans Fat 0g); Cholesterol 0mg; Sodium 380mg; Total Carbohydrate 51g (Dietary Fiber 4g; Sugars 6g); Protein 10g **% Daily Value:** Vitamin A 0%; Vitamin C 4%; Calcium 2%; Iron 4% **Exchanges:** 2½ Starch, 1 Other Carbohydrate **Carbohydrate Choices:** 3 ½

Rye Berries with Butternut Squash

PREP TIME: **15 MINUTES** • START TO FINISH: **15 HOURS 45 MINUTES** • **9 SIDE-DISH SERVINGS** (½ CUP EACH) •
WHOLE GRAIN SERVING: ½

1½ cups uncooked rye berries

⅓ cup water

1 can (14 oz) chicken broth

1 small onion, chopped
 (¼ cup)

1 tablespoon firm butter or
 margarine, cut into small
 pieces

½ teaspoon ground cinnamon

¼ teaspoon salt

1½ cups 1½-inch pieces peeled
 butternut squash

½ cup chopped walnuts

1　In large bowl, place rye berries; add enough water to cover. Let soak in refrigerator at least 8 hours but no longer than 24 hours; drain.

2　Spray 3- to 4-quart slow cooker with cooking spray. Place drained rye berries and remaining ingredients except squash and walnuts in slow cooker. Stir to mix.

3　Cover; cook on Low heat setting 7 to 8 hours or until rye berries are chewy but tender.

4　Stir in squash. Increase heat setting to High. Cover; cook about 30 minutes or until squash is tender. Stir in walnuts.

Betty Tip

Rye berries are native to eastern Europe, where it was a hardy crop suitable to the harsh cold and wet climate of that area; European peasants called it "black wheat." Indeed, nutritionally, it is most close to wheat, containing vitamins B and E, protein and iron.

1 Serving: Calories 290 (Calories from Fat 60); Total Fat 7g (Saturated Fat 1.5g; Trans Fat 0g); Cholesterol 0mg; Sodium 270mg; Total Carbohydrate 45g (Dietary Fiber 0g; Sugars 1g); Protein 11g **% Daily Value:** Vitamin A 45%; Vitamin C 2%; Calcium 0%; Iron 2% **Exchanges:** 3 Starch, 1 Fat **Carbohydrate Choices:** 3

salads, soups and sides

Veggies and Kasha with Balsamic
Vinaigrette *Page 174*

7

Wheat Berry Salad

PREP TIME: **10 MINUTES** • START TO FINISH: **2 HOURS 40 MINUTES** • **8 SERVINGS** • WHOLE GRAIN SERVING: ½

Wheat Berries

1 cup uncooked wheat berries

4 cups water

Creamy Vinaigrette Dressing

⅓ cup canola oil

2 tablespoons mayonnaise
  or salad dressing

2 tablespoons red wine vinegar

½ teaspoon salt

¼ teaspoon garlic powder

⅛ teaspoon pepper

Salad

1 cup chopped broccoli

1 cup chopped cauliflower

1 cup cherry tomatoes,
  cut in half

1 small green bell pepper,
  chopped (½ cup)

4 medium green onions, sliced
  (¼ cup)

½ cup crumbled reduced-fat
  feta cheese (2 oz)

1 In 3-quart saucepan, soak wheat berries in water 30 minutes. Heat to boiling over high heat. Reduce heat to low. Partially cover; simmer 55 to 60 minutes or until wheat berries are tender. Drain and rinse with cold water.

2 In small bowl, stir all dressing ingredients until well mixed.

3 In large serving bowl, toss wheat berries, salad ingredients and dressing. Cover; refrigerate at least 1 hour.

Betty Tip

Wheat berries are whole, unprocessed kernels of wheat. Look for wheat berries in the cereal, self-serve bulk foods or natural-foods section of your supermarket.

1 Serving: Calories 190 (Calories from Fat 120); Total Fat 13g (Saturated Fat 2g; Trans Fat 0g); Cholesterol 0mg; Sodium 280mg; Total Carbohydrate 14g (Dietary Fiber 3g; Sugars 2g); Protein 4g **% Daily Value:** Vitamin A 10%; Vitamin C 45%; Calcium 4%; Iron 4% **Exchanges:** 1 Starch, ½ Vegetable, 2 Fat **Carbohydrate Choices:** 1

Mediterranean Quinoa Salad

PREP TIME: **30 MINUTES** • START TO FINISH: **1 HOUR 35 MINUTES** • **4 SERVINGS** (¾ CUP EACH) • WHOLE GRAIN SERVING: **2**

1 cup uncooked quinoa

2 cups roasted garlic-seasoned chicken broth (from two 14-oz cans)

½ cup chopped drained roasted red bell peppers (from 7-oz jar)

½ cup cubed provolone cheese

¼ cup chopped kalamata olives

2 tablespoons chopped fresh basil leaves

2 tablespoons Italian dressing

1   Rinse quinoa thoroughly by placing in a fine-mesh strainer and holding under cold running water until water runs clear; drain well.

2   In 2-quart saucepan, heat quinoa and broth to boiling; reduce heat. Cover; simmer 15 to 20 minutes or until quinoa is tender. Drain quinoa. Cool completely, about 45 minutes.

3   In large serving bowl, toss quinoa and remaining ingredients. Serve immediately, or refrigerate 1 to 2 hours before serving.

Betty Tip

Quinoa is a popular grain in South American cuisine and is gaining popularity in the United States. Its nutrition profile is impressive because it is a complete protein.

1 Serving: Calories 290 (Calories from Fat 100); Total Fat 12g (Saturated Fat 3.5g; Trans Fat 0g); Cholesterol 15mg; Sodium 810mg; Total Carbohydrate 33g (Dietary Fiber 3g; Sugars 5g); Protein 13g **% Daily Value:** Vitamin A 30%; Vitamin C 35%; Calcium 15%; Iron 25% **Exchanges:** 2 Starch, 1 High-Fat Meat, ½ Fat **Carbohydrate Choices:** 2

Turkey–Wild Rice Salad

PREP TIME: **20 MINUTES** • START TO FINISH: **1 HOUR 20 MINUTES** • **4 SERVINGS** • WHOLE GRAIN SERVING: **1½**

1 cup uncooked wild rice

2½ cups water

1 lb uncooked turkey breast slices, about ¼ inch thick

¼ teaspoon seasoned salt

¼ teaspoon dried marjoram leaves

¼ cup chopped walnuts

¼ cup sweetened dried cranberries

4 medium green onions, chopped (¼ cup)

¼ teaspoon salt

½ cup fresh raspberries

4 large leaf lettuce leaves

½ cup raspberry vinaigrette dressing

1   Cook wild rice in water as directed on package, or see page 16. Place cooked wild rice in colander or strainer; rinse with cold water 5 minutes to chill.

2   Sprinkle turkey with seasoned salt and marjoram. Spray 10-inch skillet with cooking spray; heat over medium-high heat. Cook turkey in skillet 4 to 6 minutes, turning once, until no longer pink in center. Cut into 2-inch pieces.

3   In large bowl, mix cooked wild rice, walnuts, cranberries, onions and salt. Carefully stir in raspberries.

4   On 4 plates, arrange lettuce leaves. Top with rice mixture. Arrange warm turkey on rice mixture. Drizzle with dressing.

Betty Tip

Make it easier on yourself by preparing the wild rice one night and letting it chill, then adding the rest of the ingredients the next night when you serve this salad.

1 Serving: Calories 390 (Calories from Fat 60); Total Fat 7g (Saturated Fat 1g; Trans Fat 0g); Cholesterol 75mg; Sodium 650mg; Total Carbohydrate 48g (Dietary Fiber 5g; Sugars 12g); Protein 34g **% Daily Value:** Vitamin A 20%; Vitamin C 15%; Calcium 4%; Iron 15% **Exchanges:** 2 Starch, 1 Other Carbohydrate, 4 Very Lean Meat, ½ Fat **Carbohydrate Choices:** 3

Creamy Rice-Fruit Salad

PREP TIME: **15 MINUTES** • START TO FINISH: **1 HOUR 15 MINUTES** • **8 SERVINGS** • WHOLE GRAIN SERVING: ½

⅔ cup uncooked wild rice

1⅔ cups water

1 container (8 oz) lemon or orange low-fat yogurt

1 tablespoon honey

1 cup fresh strawberries, cut in half

½ cup seedless green grapes, cut in half

1 kiwifruit, peeled, cut into ¼-inch slices, slices cut into quarters

1 medium seedless orange, cut into 1-inch pieces (1 cup)

1 teaspoon chopped fresh or ¼ teaspoon dried mint leaves

1   Cook wild rice in water as directed on package, or see page 16. Place cooked wild rice in colander or strainer; rinse with cold water 5 minutes to chill.

2   In medium bowl, mix yogurt and honey. Add cooked wild rice and remaining ingredients; toss.

Betty Tip

If you like brown rice, you can substitute that for the wild rice. Or use a combination of brown rice and wild rice for a great taste and appearance.

1 Serving: Calories 120 (Calories from Fat 5); Total Fat 0.5g (Saturated Fat 0g; Trans Fat 0g); Cholesterol 0mg; Sodium 20mg; Total Carbohydrate 24g (Dietary Fiber 2g; Sugars 11g); Protein 4g
% Daily Value: Vitamin A 0%; Vitamin C 50%; Calcium 6%; Iron 2% **Exchanges:** 1 Starch, ½ Fruit **Carbohydrate Choices:** 1½

Harvest Salad

PREP TIME: **20 MINUTES** • START TO FINISH: **40 MINUTES** • **8 SERVINGS** • WHOLE GRAIN SERVING: **1**

1 cup uncooked quick-cooking barley

2 cups water

2 cups frozen whole kernel corn, thawed, drained

½ cup sweetened dried cranberries

4 medium green onions, thinly sliced (¼ cup)

1 medium unpeeled apple, chopped (1 cup)

1 small carrot, coarsely shredded (⅓ cup)

2 tablespoons canola oil

2 tablespoons honey

1 tablespoon lemon juice

1   Cook barley in water as directed on package, or see page 16.

2   In large bowl, mix cooked barley, corn, cranberries, onions, apple and carrot.

3   In tightly covered container, shake oil, honey and lemon juice. Pour over barley mixture; toss.

Betty Tip

Quick-cooking barley contains the nutrients of regular barley in a convenient, time-saving form. Combining grains, fruits and vegetables makes an interesting and good-for-you salad, one that's colorful and fancy enough to serve to company, yet easy enough to make for just you and your family.

1 Serving: Calories 240 (Calories from Fat 40); Total Fat 4g (Saturated Fat 0g; Trans Fat 0g); Cholesterol 0mg; Sodium 10mg; Total Carbohydrate 45g (Dietary Fiber 7g; Sugars 13g); Protein 4g **% Daily Value:** Vitamin A 15%; Vitamin C 6%; Calcium 0%; Iron 6% **Exchanges:** 1½ Starch, 1½ Other Carbohydrate, ½ Fat **Carbohydrate Choices:** 3

Tarragon-Couscous Salad

PREP TIME: **25 MINUTES** • START TO FINISH: **55 MINUTES** • **6 SERVINGS** (1 CUP EACH) • WHOLE GRAIN SERVING: **1**

3⅓ cups water

½ cup dried red lentils, sorted, rinsed

2 teaspoons olive oil

¼ teaspoon salt

1 cup uncooked whole wheat couscous (from 11-oz box)

3 tablespoons olive oil

3 tablespoons seasoned rice vinegar

1 teaspoon Dijon mustard

1 clove garlic, finely chopped

1 medium carrot, finely chopped (½ cup)

4 medium green onions, finely chopped (¼ cup)

¼ cup chopped walnuts, toasted (page 17)

2 tablespoons chopped fresh parsley

1 tablespoon chopped fresh or 1 teaspoon crushed dried tarragon leaves

1 In 1-quart saucepan, heat 2 cups of the water to boiling. Stir in lentils; reduce heat to low. Cook 10 to 12 minutes or until just tender. Drain; cool 15 minutes.

2 Meanwhile, in 1-quart saucepan, heat remaining 1⅓ cups water, 2 teaspoons oil and the salt to boiling. Stir in couscous; remove from heat. Cover; let stand 5 minutes. Fluff couscous lightly with fork. Cool 10 minutes.

3 Meanwhile, in medium bowl, beat 3 tablespoons oil, the vinegar, mustard and garlic with wire whisk until blended. Stir in carrot, onions, walnuts, parsley and tarragon. Stir in lentils and couscous. Serve immediately or refrigerate until serving.

Betty Tip

Now you can get whole wheat couscous, whole-grain pasta buds that look so close to regular couscous, the kids will never know the difference. Tarragon is a nice touch with mild-tasting couscous, but cut back a bit if it is not your favorite flavor. Or you can double the amount of parsley and leave out the tarragon altogether.

1 Serving: Calories 290 (Calories from Fat 110); Total Fat 12g (Saturated Fat 1.5g; Trans Fat 0g); Cholesterol 0mg; Sodium 130mg; Total Carbohydrate 35g (Dietary Fiber 6g; Sugars 1g); Protein 9g
% Daily Value: Vitamin A 30%; Vitamin C 6%; Calcium 4%; Iron 15% **Exchanges:** 2½ Starch, 2 Fat
Carbohydrate Choices: 2

Rye Berry Borscht

PREP TIME: **30 MINUTES** • START TO FINISH: **10 HOURS 45 MINUTES** • **8 SERVINGS** (1²/₃ CUPS EACH) • WHOLE GRAIN SERVING: ½

1 cup uncooked rye berries

4 cups water

3 cups chopped green cabbage

6 medium beets (about 1¼ lb), peeled, chopped (3 cups)

2 medium stalks celery, chopped (1 cup)

1 medium potato, peeled, cubed (1 cup)

1 medium carrot, chopped (½ cup)

1 medium onion, chopped (½ cup)

2 cloves garlic, finely chopped

1 can (28 oz) diced tomatoes, undrained

4 cups water

1 can (19 oz) cannellini beans, drained, rinsed

3 tablespoons honey

1½ teaspoons salt

½ teaspoon caraway seed

¼ teaspoon pepper

1 In 5-quart nonstick Dutch oven, soak rye berries in 4 cups water in refrigerator at least 8 hours but no longer than 24 hours.

2 Heat rye berries in water to boiling over high heat. Reduce heat to low. Cover; simmer about 45 minutes or until chewy but tender. Drain.

3 In same Dutch oven, heat cooked rye berries, cabbage, beets, celery, potato, carrot, onion, garlic, tomatoes and 4 cups water to boiling over high heat. Reduce heat to low. Cover; cook 45 minutes.

4 Stir in beans, honey, salt, caraway seed and pepper. Cover; cook 30 to 45 minutes until vegetables are tender.

Betty Tip

The rye berries are a nice complement to the hardy flavors of the cabbage and beets. Make it easy on yourself by using 3½ cups purchased coleslaw mix in place of the chopped cabbage and carrot.

1 Serving: Calories 350 (Calories from Fat 15); Total Fat 1.5g (Saturated Fat 0g; Trans Fat 0g); Cholesterol 0mg; Sodium 640mg; Total Carbohydrate 69g (Dietary Fiber 7g; Sugars 16g); Protein 15g **% Daily Value:** Vitamin A 25%; Vitamin C 20%; Calcium 10%; Iron 20% **Exchanges:** 3 Starch, 1 Other Carbohydrate, 1 Vegetable, ½ Very Lean Meat **Carbohydrate Choices:** 4 ½

Veggies and Kasha with Balsamic Vinaigrette

PREP TIME: **15 MINUTES** • START TO FINISH: **2 HOURS 20 MINUTES** • **4 SERVINGS (1 CUP EACH)** • WHOLE GRAIN SERVING: ½

Salad

1 cup water

½ cup uncooked buckwheat kernels or groats (kasha)

4 medium green onions, thinly sliced (¼ cup)

2 medium tomatoes, seeded, coarsely chopped (1½ cups)

1 medium unpeeled cucumber, seeded, chopped (1¼ cups)

Vinaigrette

2 tablespoons balsamic or red wine vinegar

1 tablespoon olive oil

2 teaspoons sugar

½ teaspoon salt

¼ teaspoon pepper

1 clove garlic, finely chopped

1   In 8-inch skillet, heat water to boiling. Add kasha; cook over medium-high heat 7 to 8 minutes, stirring occasionally, until tender. Drain if necessary.

2   In large bowl, mix kasha and remaining salad ingredients.

3   In tightly covered container, shake all vinaigrette ingredients until blended. Pour vinaigrette over kasha mixture; toss. Cover; refrigerate 1 to 2 hours to blend flavors.

Betty Tip

The color and crunch of the vegetables and the chewiness of the kasha create a salad that looks and tastes wonderful, perfect for family and friends.

1 Serving: Calories 120 (Calories from Fat 35); Total Fat 4g (Saturated Fat 0.5g; Trans Fat 0g); Cholesterol 0mg; Sodium 300mg; Total Carbohydrate 18g (Dietary Fiber 3g; Sugars 5g); Protein 3g **% Daily Value:** Vitamin A 15%; Vitamin C 20%; Calcium 2%; Iron 4% **Exchanges:** ½ Starch, ½ Other Carbohydrate, 1 Vegetable, ½ Fat **Carbohydrate Choices:** 1

Savory Millet and Potato Stew

PREP TIME: **35 MINUTES** • START TO FINISH: **35 MINUTES** • **6 SERVINGS** (ABOUT 1⅓ CUPS EACH) • WHOLE GRAIN SERVING: ½

5 cups reduced-sodium chicken broth

2 tablespoons soy sauce

1 bag (1 lb) frozen broccoli, carrots and cauliflower (or other combination)

1 cup diced red potatoes

1 cup uncooked millet

1 teaspoon dried thyme leaves

¼ to ½ teaspoon pepper

1 large onion, chopped (1 cup)

4 cloves garlic, finely chopped

1 In 4-quart saucepan or Dutch oven, heat broth and soy sauce to boiling. Stir in remaining ingredients.

2 Heat to boiling; reduce heat to medium. Cover; cook 12 to 16 minutes, stirring occasionally, until millet and potatoes are tender.

Betty Tip

Thick and rich tasting, millet is a tiny, high-protein, low-fat whole grain that cooks in just a few minutes. Whole grains are concentrated sources of nutrients and phytochemicals, thought to have heart- and health-protective benefits.

1 Serving: Calories 200 (Calories from Fat 15); Total Fat 1.5g (Saturated Fat 0g; Trans Fat 0g); Cholesterol 0mg; Sodium 790mg; Total Carbohydrate 37g (Dietary Fiber 6g; Sugars 3g); Protein 9g **% Daily Value:** Vitamin A 35%; Vitamin C 25%; Calcium 6%; Iron 15% **Exchanges:** 2 Starch, 1 Vegetable **Carbohydrate Choices:** 2½

Chicken Creole Soup

PREP TIME: **20 MINUTES** • START TO FINISH: **1 HOUR 10 MINUTES** • **8 SERVINGS** (1¾ CUPS EACH) • WHOLE GRAIN SERVING: ½

2 tablespoons butter or margarine

2 medium onions, coarsely chopped (1 cup)

2 medium stalks celery, coarsely chopped (1 cup)

1 medium green bell pepper, coarsely chopped (1 cup)

2 teaspoons finely chopped garlic

2½ lb boneless skinless chicken breasts, cut into 1-inch pieces

4 cups chicken broth

2 cups water

2 cans (14.5 oz each) diced tomatoes, undrained

1 cup uncooked long-grain brown rice

½ teaspoon salt

¼ teaspoon ground red pepper (cayenne)

2 dried bay leaves

1 In 5- to 6-quart Dutch oven, melt butter over medium-high heat. Add onions, celery, bell pepper, garlic and chicken; cook 7 to 9 minutes, stirring frequently, until onions are softened and chicken is no longer pink in center.

2 Stir in remaining ingredients. Heat to boiling; reduce heat to medium-low. Cover; cook 40 to 45 minutes, stirring occasionally, until rice is tender.

3 Remove bay leaves before serving.

Betty Tip

You can mix and match your grains. Creole is usually made with rice, but if you have barley on hand, use that instead of brown rice for a change. Once you get used to various grains and their cook times, you'll find mixing and matching grains adds interest to your cooking.

1 Serving: Calories 330 (Calories from Fat 80); Total Fat 9g (Saturated Fat 3.5g; Trans Fat 0g); Cholesterol 95mg; Sodium 900mg; Total Carbohydrate 26g (Dietary Fiber 4g; Sugars 4g); Protein 37g **% Daily Value:** Vitamin A 8%; Vitamin C 20%; Calcium 8%; Iron 15% **Exchanges:** 1½ Starch, 1 Vegetable, 4 Very Lean Meat, 1 Fat **Carbohydrate Choices:** 2

Barley-Burger Stew

PREP TIME: **15 MINUTES** • START TO FINISH: **1 HOUR 20 MINUTES** • **4 SERVINGS** • WHOLE GRAIN SERVING: **½**

1 lb extra-lean (at least 90%) ground beef

2 medium onions, chopped (1 cup)

½ cup uncooked hulled or pearl barley

1 cup water

2 to 3 teaspoons chili powder

½ teaspoon salt

½ teaspoon pepper

1 medium stalk celery, chopped (½ cup)

4 cups tomato juice

1 In 4-quart Dutch oven, cook beef and onions over medium heat 8 to 10 minutes, stirring occasionally, until beef is thoroughly cooked; drain.

2 Stir remaining ingredients into beef mixture. Heat to boiling; reduce heat. Cover; simmer about 1 hour or until barley is tender and stew is desired consistency.

Betty Tip

Just 1 cup of cooked barley packs about 6 grams of fiber. This virtually fat-free whole grain also contains complex carbohydrates, B vitamins and protein. This stew, reminiscent of chili, is also great if you add 1 can of rinsed and drained kidney beans.

1 Serving: Calories 330 (Calories from Fat 90); Total Fat 10g (Saturated Fat 4g; Trans Fat 0.5g); Cholesterol 70mg; Sodium 1030mg; Total Carbohydrate 35g (Dietary Fiber 6g; Sugars 10g); Protein 27g **% Daily Value:** Vitamin A 30%; Vitamin C 40%; Calcium 6%; Iron 25% **Exchanges:** ½ Starch, 1 Other Carbohydrate, 2 Vegetable, 3 Lean Meat **Carbohydrate Choices:** 2

Red Harvest Quinoa

PREP TIME: **20 MINUTES** • START TO FINISH: **40 MINUTES** • **8 SERVINGS** (½ CUP EACH) • WHOLE GRAIN SERVING: **1**

1 cup uncooked red or white quinoa

1 tablespoon butter or margarine

¼ cup chopped red onion

⅓ cup chopped celery

½ cup coarsely chopped baking apple

1½ cups roasted vegetable stock (from 32-oz container) or chicken broth

½ cup orange juice

½ cup sweetened dried cranberries

1 jar (1¾ oz) pine nuts (about ⅓ cup), toasted (page 17)

¼ cup shredded Parmesan cheese (1 oz)

¼ teaspoon salt

2 tablespoons finely chopped parsley

1   Rinse quinoa thoroughly by placing in a fine-mesh strainer and holding under cold running water until water runs clear; drain well.

2   In 2-quart saucepan, melt butter over medium heat. Cook onion, celery, apple and quinoa in butter 5 minutes, stirring occasionally.

3   Stir in vegetable stock and orange juice. Heat to boiling; reduce heat. Cover; simmer 15 to 20 minutes or until all liquid is absorbed and quinoa is tender. Fluff with fork.

4   Stir in cranberries, nuts, cheese and salt. Sprinkle with parsley.

Betty Tip

Once you're used to eating grains, you'll want to serve them often. Quinoa is high in protein, low in fat and cooks quickly, making it a great grain to use. The cranberries, orange juice and apple are reminiscent of fall. If you'd like to reduce the saturated fat, use canola oil instead of butter.

1 Serving: Calories 190 (Calories from Fat 70); Total Fat 8g (Saturated Fat 2g; Trans Fat 0g); Cholesterol 5mg; Sodium 340mg; Total Carbohydrate 26g (Dietary Fiber 2g; Sugars 10g); Protein 5g **% Daily Value:** Vitamin A 8%; Vitamin C 8%; Calcium 6%; Iron 15% **Exchanges:** 1½ Starch, 1½ Fat **Carbohydrate Choices:** 2

Creamy Quinoa Primavera

PREP TIME: **20 MINUTES** • START TO FINISH: **35 MINUTES** • **6 SERVINGS** • WHOLE GRAIN SERVING: **2**

1½ cups uncooked quinoa

3 cups chicken broth

2 teaspoons canola oil

2 cloves garlic, finely chopped

5 cups assorted vegetables, thinly sliced or bite-size pieces (such as asparagus, broccoli, carrot and zucchini)

3 oz (from 8-oz package) ⅓-less-fat cream cheese (Neufchâtel)

1 tablespoon chopped fresh or 1 teaspoon dried basil leaves

2 tablespoons grated Romano cheese

1 In colander or strainer, rinse quinoa thoroughly; drain. In 2-quart saucepan, heat quinoa and broth to boiling; reduce heat. Cover; simmer 10 to 15 minutes or until all broth is absorbed.

2 Meanwhile, in 12-inch nonstick skillet, heat oil over medium-high heat. Cook garlic in oil about 30 seconds, stirring frequently, until golden. Stir in vegetables. Cook about 5 minutes, stirring frequently, until vegetables are crisp-tender.

3 Stir cream cheese and basil into quinoa. Add quinoa mixture to vegetables; toss. Sprinkle with Romano cheese.

Betty Tip

One technique to add more flavor to grains is to cook and stir them in a little butter or oil on the stove-top. This "toasts" the grain, so the flavors pop more. You can try that in this dish: Drain the quinoa, cook and stir it in a little melted butter for a few minutes, then add the rest of the ingredients.

1 Serving: Calories 270 (Calories from Fat 80); Total Fat 9g (Saturated Fat 3g; Trans Fat 0g); Cholesterol 15mg; Sodium 620mg; Total Carbohydrate 34g (Dietary Fiber 4g; Sugars 4g); Protein 12g
% Daily Value: Vitamin A 15%; Vitamin C 30%; Calcium 10%; Iron 25% **Exchanges:** 2 Starch, 1 Vegetable, ½ Medium-Fat Meat, 1 Fat **Carbohydrate Choices:** 2

Onion and Mushroom Quinoa

PREP TIME: **15 MINUTES** • START TO FINISH: **30 MINUTES** • **6 SERVINGS** • WHOLE GRAIN SERVING: **1**

1 cup uncooked quinoa

1 teaspoon canola oil

1 small onion, cut into fourths, then sliced

1 medium carrot, shredded (⅔ cup)

1 small green bell pepper, chopped (½ cup)

1 cup sliced mushrooms (3 oz)

1 teaspoon chopped fresh or ¼ teaspoon dried thyme leaves

¼ teaspoon salt

1 can (14 oz) vegetable or chicken broth

1 Rinse quinoa thoroughly by placing in a fine-mesh strainer and holding under cold running water until water runs clear; drain well.

2 In 2-quart saucepan, heat oil over medium heat. Cook quinoa and onion in oil 4 to 5 minutes, stirring occasionally, until light brown.

3 Stir in remaining ingredients. Heat to boiling; reduce heat. Cover; simmer about 15 minutes or until liquid is absorbed. Fluff with fork.

Betty Tip

Quinoa has been hailed as a "supergrain" because it contains more protein than any other grain. Tiny and bead-shaped, ivory-colored quinoa takes only 20 minutes to cook. Like other whole grains, it's low in fat and provides a rich, balanced source of vital nutrients.

1 Serving: Calories 140 (Calories from Fat 25); Total Fat 2.5g (Saturated Fat 0g; Trans Fat 0g); Cholesterol 0mg; Sodium 390mg; Total Carbohydrate 24g (Dietary Fiber 3g; Sugars 4g); Protein 4g **% Daily Value:** Vitamin A 35%; Vitamin C 10%; Calcium 2%; Iron 15% **Exchanges:** 1 Starch, ½ Other Carbohydrate, ½ Fat **Carbohydrate Choices:** 1½

Lemon-Parsley Three-Grain Pilaf

PREP TIME: **10 MINUTES** • START TO FINISH: **1 HOUR** • **6 SERVINGS** (ABOUT ½ CUP EACH) • WHOLE GRAIN SERVING: ½

1 can (14 oz) chicken broth

¾ cup water

¼ teaspoon onion powder

½ cup uncooked long-grain brown rice

½ cup uncooked millet

½ cup frozen whole kernel corn

½ cup coarsely chopped fresh parsley

1 teaspoon grated lemon peel

1 In 2-quart saucepan, heat broth, water and onion powder to boiling. Stir in rice; reduce heat to low. Cover; cook 15 minutes.

2 Stir in millet. Cover; cook 25 to 30 minutes or until most of liquid is absorbed.

3 Stir in corn. Cover; cook 5 minutes. Stir in parsley and lemon peel. Serve immediately.

Betty Tip

This pilaf looks and tastes very fresh. The corn, lemon and parsley add wonderful flavor, and the millet and brown rice add a nice texture and are truly great together. Experiment with other combinations of grains; if the cook times aren't similar, either start one first or choose grains that cook in the same amount of time.

1 Serving: Calories 140 (Calories from Fat 15); Total Fat 1.5g (Saturated Fat 0g; Trans Fat 0g); Cholesterol 0mg; Sodium 290mg; Total Carbohydrate 27g (Dietary Fiber 4g; Sugars 0g); Protein 5g **% Daily Value:** Vitamin A 10%; Vitamin C 6%; Calcium 0%; Iron 6% **Exchanges:** 2 Starch **Carbohydrate Choices:** 2

Brown Rice Pilaf with Pea Pods

PREP TIME: **15 MINUTES** • START TO FINISH: **1 HOUR** • **6 SERVINGS** (⅔ CUP EACH) • WHOLE GRAIN SERVING: **1**

1 can (14 oz) chicken broth

½ cup water

1 teaspoon dried thyme leaves

1 cup uncooked long-grain brown rice

1 teaspoon canola oil

½ cup finely chopped red bell pepper

½ cup sugar snap pea pods, cut into ¾-inch pieces

⅓ cup sliced green onions (about 5 medium)

1   In 2-quart saucepan, heat broth, water and thyme to boiling. Stir in rice. Cover; simmer 45 to 50 minutes or until rice is tender.

2   Meanwhile, in 8-inch skillet, heat oil over medium-high heat. Cook bell pepper, pea pods and onions in oil 3 to 4 minutes, stirring frequently, until tender.

3   When rice is cooked, stir pea pod mixture into rice.

Betty Tip

Brown rice, rich in fiber and flavor, takes longer to cook than white rice, so allow 45 to 50 minutes for cooking. Serve this rice pilaf with your favorite fish or seafood recipe. Include a citrus fruit salad and whole-grain bread.

1 Serving: Calories 140 (Calories from Fat 20); Total Fat 2g (Saturated Fat 0g; Trans Fat 0g); Cholesterol 0mg; Sodium 290mg; Total Carbohydrate 26g (Dietary Fiber 4g; Sugars 1g); Protein 4g
% Daily Value: Vitamin A 10%; Vitamin C 25%; Calcium 2%; Iron 6% **Exchanges:** 1½ Starch, ½ Fat
Carbohydrate Choices: 2

Red Pepper Polenta with Gorgonzola

PREP TIME: **45 MINUTES** • START TO FINISH: **1 HOUR** • **8 SERVINGS** • WHOLE GRAIN SERVING: **1**

2 teaspoons olive oil

2 cloves garlic, finely chopped

½ cup coarsely chopped red
 bell pepper

2 cups roasted vegetable stock
 (from 32-oz container)
 or chicken broth

1 cup milk

1 cup whole-grain yellow
 cornmeal

½ teaspoon salt

½ cup crumbled Gorgonzola
 cheese (2 oz)

1   In 2-quart saucepan, heat oil over medium heat. Cook garlic and bell pepper in oil about 2 minutes, stirring occasionally, until bell pepper is crisp-tender.

2   Stir in vegetable stock and milk; heat to boiling. Gradually stir in cornmeal and salt; reduce heat to low. Simmer uncovered about 30 minutes, stirring frequently, until slightly thickened.

3   Spray 10-inch pie plate with cooking spray. Pour polenta into pie plate. Sprinkle with cheese. Let stand about 10 minutes or until cheese is melted and polenta is firm enough to cut. Cut into 8 wedges.

Betty Tip

Cornmeal makes a soft, tender polenta; stir it in slowly to avoid lumps. The Gorgonzola cheese and red pepper are dynamite together!

1 Serving: Calories 120 (Calories from Fat 35); Total Fat 4g (Saturated Fat 2g; Trans Fat 0g); Cholesterol 10mg; Sodium 510mg; Total Carbohydrate 17g (Dietary Fiber 0g; Sugars 3g); Protein 4g
% Daily Value: Vitamin A 15%; Vitamin C 15%; Calcium 8%; Iron 4% **Exchanges:** 1 Starch, 1 Fat
Carbohydrate Choices: 1

Polenta Sauté

PREP TIME: **35 MINUTES** • START TO FINISH: **1 HOUR 50 MINUTES** • **4 SERVINGS** • WHOLE GRAIN SERVING: **2**

1 cup frozen whole kernel corn

4 cups water

1 teaspoon butter or margarine

½ teaspoon salt

¼ teaspoon pepper

1 cup whole-grain cornmeal

1 Spray 11 × 7-inch (2-quart) glass baking dish with cooking spray. In 2-quart saucepan, heat all ingredients except cornmeal to boiling. Gradually add cornmeal, stirring constantly. Reduce heat to medium-low. Cook 8 to 12 minutes, stirring occasionally, until mixture pulls away from side of saucepan.

2 Pour polenta into baking dish. Cool 15 minutes. Cover; refrigerate about 1 hour or until firm.

3 Heat oven to 250°F. Cut polenta into 8 pieces. Spray 10-inch skillet with cooking spray; heat over medium heat. Cook 4 pieces of polenta at a time in skillet about 5 minutes on each side or until light brown. Place on ungreased cookie sheet; keep warm in oven while cooking remaining pieces.

Betty Tip

Doubly delicious with both whole kernel corn and cornmeal, this easy side dish can be made with either yellow or white cornmeal. Serve polenta with salsa, reduced-fat sour cream and some sliced ripe olives.

1 Serving: Calories 170 (Calories from Fat 15); Total Fat 2g (Saturated Fat 0.5g; Trans Fat 0g); Cholesterol 0mg; Sodium 310mg; Total Carbohydrate 34g (Dietary Fiber 2g; Sugars 1g); Protein 4g **% Daily Value:** Vitamin A 4%; Vitamin C 0%; Calcium 0%; Iron 10% **Exchanges:** 2 Starch **Carbohydrate Choices:** 2

Granola-Topped Sweet Potatoes

PREP TIME: **25 MINUTES** • START TO FINISH: **1 HOUR 20 MINUTES** • **8 SERVINGS** (½ CUP EACH) • WHOLE GRAIN SERVING: ½

6 medium dark-orange sweet potatoes, peeled, cut into 1½-inch pieces (7 to 8 cups)

½ cup evaporated milk (from 5-oz can)

1 tablespoon butter or margarine

¼ cup real maple syrup or maple-flavored syrup

½ teaspoon salt

6 maple-brown sugar crunchy granola bars (3 pouches from 8.9-oz box), crushed

1 tablespoon butter or margarine, melted

1 In 4-quart saucepan, place potato pieces and add enough water to cover. Heat to boiling; reduce heat to medium-low. Cook uncovered 15 to 20 minutes or until tender. Drain and return to saucepan.

2 Heat oven to 350°F. Spray 8-inch square (2-quart) glass baking dish with cooking spray. To potatoes, add evaporated milk, butter, the maple syrup and salt. Mash with potato masher or electric mixer until smooth. Spoon into baking dish. In small bowl, mix crushed granola bars and 1 tablespoon melted butter; sprinkle over potatoes.

3 Bake uncovered 25 to 30 minutes or until thoroughly heated and topping is crisp.

Betty Tip

You can make this rich-tasting casserole up to 8 hours ahead of time, but wait to sprinkle with the granola bar mixture until just before baking.

1 Serving: Calories 250 (Calories from Fat 50); Total Fat 6g (Saturated Fat 2.5g; Trans Fat 0g); Cholesterol 10mg; Sodium 290mg; Total Carbohydrate 44g (Dietary Fiber 5g; Sugars 23g); Protein 5g **% Daily Value:** Vitamin A 450%; Vitamin C 20%; Calcium 10%; Iron 8% **Exchanges:** 1½ Starch, 1½ Other Carbohydrate, 1 Fat **Carbohydrate Choices:** 3

Herb Barley and Asparagus

PREP TIME: **20 MINUTES** • START TO FINISH: **1 HOUR** • **8 SERVINGS** (½ CUP EACH) • WHOLE GRAIN SERVING: ½

2 cans (14 oz each) chicken broth

1 cup uncooked hulled barley

1 tablespoon canola oil

1 medium onion, chopped (½ cup)

1 medium carrot, chopped (½ cup)

8 oz asparagus (8 to 10 stalks), cut into 1-inch pieces

¼ teaspoon dried marjoram or thyme leaves

⅛ teaspoon pepper

2 tablespoons shredded Parmesan cheese

1 In 2-quart saucepan, heat broth to boiling. Stir in barley. Reduce heat to low; cover and simmer 50 minutes.

2 About 5 minutes before barley is done, in 12-inch skillet, heat oil over medium heat. Cook onion and carrot in oil 3 to 4 minutes, stirring occasionally, until crisp-tender.

3 Stir barley, asparagus, marjoram and pepper into cooked onion mixture. Cover; cook 7 to 8 minutes, stirring occasionally, until barley is tender and liquid is absorbed. Stir in cheese.

Betty Tip

To boost the flavor when cooking with grains, a trick of the trade is to cook them in broth (chicken, beef or vegetable), apple juice or vegetable juice.

1 Serving: Calories 140 (Calories from Fat 30); Total Fat 3g (Saturated Fat 0.5g; Trans Fat 0g); Cholesterol 0mg; Sodium 460mg; Total Carbohydrate 22g (Dietary Fiber 5g; Sugars 2g); Protein 6g
% Daily Value: Vitamin A 25%; Vitamin C 6%; Calcium 4%; Iron 6% **Exchanges:** 1 Starch, 1 Vegetable, ½ Fat **Carbohydrate Choices:** 1½

delicious desserts

8

Double Chocolate-
Kasha Torte *Page 209*

Raspberry-Barley Pudding

PREP TIME: **25 MINUTES** • START TO FINISH: **3 HOURS 35 MINUTES** • **6 SERVINGS** (¾ CUP EACH) • WHOLE GRAIN SERVING: ½

1¾ cups water

½ cup uncooked hulled barley

1 container (6 oz) French vanilla
low-fat yogurt

¼ cup maple-flavored syrup

1 cup frozen (thawed) reduced-
fat whipped topping

⅓ cup chopped walnuts,
toasted (page 17)

½ teaspoon ground cinnamon

1 cup fresh or frozen (thawed
and drained) raspberries

Dash ground cinnamon

Additional chopped walnuts,
if desired

1 In 2-quart saucepan, heat water to boiling. Stir in barley; reduce heat. Cover; simmer 1 hour or until tender. Cool completely, about 30 minutes.

2 In medium bowl, mix yogurt and maple syrup. Gently stir in whipped topping. Stir in barley, walnuts and ½ teaspoon ground cinnamon. Cover; refrigerate 2 hours.

3 Stir raspberries into pudding. Sprinkle pudding with dash of cinnamon and additional walnuts before serving.

Betty Tip

Remember rice pudding? Well, this is even better, with more texture and chewiness, plus the goodness of barley. Instead of the raspberries, you can try other fresh fruits, like blueberries or sliced strawberries, in this creamy pudding.

1 Serving: Calories 210 (Calories from Fat 60); Total Fat 7g (Saturated Fat 2g; Trans Fat 0g); Cholesterol 0mg; Sodium 45mg; Total Carbohydrate 34g (Dietary Fiber 4g; Sugars 12g); Protein 5g **% Daily Value:** Vitamin A 0%; Vitamin C 4%; Calcium 8%; Iron 4% **Exchanges:** 1 Starch, 1 Other Carbohydrate, ½ High-Fat Meat, ½ Fat **Carbohydrate Choices:** 2

Maple Corn Pudding

PREP TIME: **35 MINUTES** • START TO FINISH: **4 HOURS 5 MINUTES** • **8 SERVINGS** (½ CUP EACH) • WHOLE GRAIN SERVING: ½

½ cup maple-flavored syrup

1 teaspoon ground cinnamon

½ teaspoon ground ginger

¼ teaspoon ground nutmeg

¼ teaspoon salt

4 cups milk

½ cup whole-grain yellow cornmeal

½ cup mild-flavor (light) molasses

2 tablespoons butter or margarine

2 eggs, beaten

5 cups boiling water

Whipped cream, if desired

1 Heat oven to 350°F. Spray 2-quart casserole with cooking spray. In small bowl, mix maple syrup, cinnamon, ginger, nutmeg and salt until well blended; set aside.

2 In 3-quart saucepan, heat milk over medium heat just until tiny bubbles form at the edge (do not boil); stir in cornmeal. Cook over medium-low heat about 20 minutes, stirring constantly, until very thick; remove from heat. Stir in maple syrup mixture, molasses, butter and eggs.

3 Pour mixture into casserole. Place casserole in 13 × 9-inch pan on oven rack. Pour boiling water into pan until 1 inch deep. Bake 1 hour 20 minutes to 1 hour 30 minutes or until knife inserted halfway between center and edge comes out clean. Carefully remove from water; place on cooling rack. Cool completely, about 2 hours. Serve with whipped cream.

Betty Tip

You can make this authentic Native American cornmeal pudding ahead of time and store it in the refrigerator. Serve cold, or to reheat, place individual servings on small plates and heat uncovered in the microwave on Medium for 30 to 40 seconds or until warm. Raisins or currants are a nice addition—to add them, stir in with the eggs.

1 Serving: Calories 260 (Calories from Fat 60); Total Fat 7g (Saturated Fat 4g; Trans Fat 0g); Cholesterol 70mg; Sodium 190mg; Total Carbohydrate 44g (Dietary Fiber 0g; Sugars 25g); Protein 6g **% Daily Value:** Vitamin A 8%; Vitamin C 0%; Calcium 20%; Iron 10% **Exchanges:** ½ Starch, 2 Other Carbohydrate, ½ Low-Fat Milk, 1 Fat **Carbohydrate Choices:** 3

Chocolate Fudge–Raspberry Crisp

PREP TIME: **15 MINUTES** • START TO FINISH: **1 HOUR 10 MINUTES** • **9 SERVINGS** (⅔ CUP EACH) • WHOLE GRAIN SERVING: **½**

1 can (21 oz) raspberry pie filling

2 cups fresh or frozen (thawed) raspberries

½ cup packed brown sugar

½ cup whole wheat flour

½ cup old-fashioned oats

¼ cup unsweetened baking cocoa

⅓ cup butter or margarine, cut into pieces

¼ cup miniature semisweet chocolate chips

Vanilla reduced-fat ice cream, if desired

1   Heat oven to 350°F. In ungreased 8-inch square (2-quart) glass baking dish, gently stir together pie filling and raspberries.

2   In medium bowl, mix brown sugar, flour, oats and cocoa. Cut in butter, using pastry blender (or pulling 2 table knives through ingredients in opposite directions), until mixture looks like coarse crumbs. Stir in chocolate chips. Sprinkle over raspberry mixture.

3   Bake 40 to 50 minutes or until juices bubble. Cool 15 minutes. Serve warm topped with ice cream.

Betty Tip

Chocolate and fruit lovers will delight in this delicious dessert that combines two whole grains: old-fashioned oats and whole wheat flour. Be prepared to share the recipe.

1 Serving: Calories 270 (Calories from Fat 80); Total Fat 9g (Saturated Fat 5g; Trans Fat 0g); Cholesterol 20mg; Sodium 55mg; Total Carbohydrate 43g (Dietary Fiber 5g; Sugars 29g); Protein 3g **% Daily Value:** Vitamin A 4%; Vitamin C 6%; Calcium 4%; Iron 8% **Exchanges:** 1 Starch, 2 Other Carbohydrate, 1½ Fat **Carbohydrate Choices:** 3

Blueberry-Rhubarb Crisp

PREP TIME: **20 MINUTES** • START TO FINISH: **1 HOUR 30 MINUTES** • **6 SERVINGS** (½ CUP EACH) • WHOLE GRAIN SERVING: ½

2 cups Honey Nut Clusters® cereal

¾ cup packed brown sugar

⅓ cup whole wheat flour

1 teaspoon grated lemon peel

1 teaspoon ground cinnamon

¼ teaspoon ground nutmeg

4 cups chopped fresh rhubarb

1 cup fresh blueberries

¼ cup chopped pecans

1 Heat oven to 375°F. Spray bottom and sides of 8-inch square (2-quart) glass baking dish with cooking spray. Place cereal in resealable food-storage plastic bag or between sheets of waxed paper; slightly crush with rolling pin. Set aside.

2 In large bowl, mix brown sugar, flour, lemon peel, cinnamon and nutmeg. Stir in rhubarb and blueberries. Spoon into baking dish. Sprinkle with crushed cereal and pecans.

3 Bake 30 to 40 minutes or until rhubarb is tender when pierced with a fork. Let stand 30 minutes before serving.

Betty Tip

If the blueberries you're using are rather tart, add 1 tablespoon additional brown sugar.

1 Serving: Calories 270 (Calories from Fat 40); Total Fat 4.5g (Saturated Fat 0g; Trans Fat 0g); Cholesterol 0mg; Sodium 105mg; Total Carbohydrate 53g (Dietary Fiber 4g; Sugars 35g); Protein 4g **% Daily Value:** Vitamin A 2%; Vitamin C 8%; Calcium 20%; Iron 15% **Exchanges:** 1 Starch, 1 Fruit, 1½ Other Carbohydrate, 1 Fat **Carbohydrate Choices:** 3 ½

Strawberry-Apricot-Oat Squares

PREP TIME: **20 MINUTES** • START TO FINISH: **2 HOURS 20 MINUTES** • **16 SERVINGS** • WHOLE GRAIN SERVING: **½**

1 cup whole wheat flour

½ cup old-fashioned or
  quick-cooking oats

½ teaspoon baking powder

½ teaspoon baking soda

¼ teaspoon salt

¾ cup packed brown sugar

¼ cup canola oil

1 teaspoon vanilla

1 egg

½ cup strawberry preserves

½ cup cut-up dried apricots

2 tablespoons old-fashioned
  or quick-cooking oats

2 teaspoons butter or
  margarine

1 Heat oven to 350°F. Spray bottom and sides of 8- or 9-inch square pan with cooking spray.

2 In large bowl, mix flour, ½ cup oats, the baking powder, baking soda and salt; set aside. In medium bowl, stir brown sugar, oil, vanilla and egg with fork until smooth; stir into flour mixture until blended. Reserve ½ cup dough in small bowl for topping.

3 Pat remaining dough in pan (if dough is sticky, spray fingers with cooking spray or lightly flour). Spread preserves over dough; sprinkle with apricots.

4 Add 2 tablespoons oats and the butter to reserved dough; mix with pastry blender or fork until crumbly. Drop small spoonfuls of oat mixture evenly over apricots.

5 Bake 25 to 28 minutes or until top is golden and firm. Cool completely, about 1 hour 30 minutes. For squares, cut into 4 rows by 4 rows.

Betty Tip

The old-fashioned oats lend a homemade appearance and texture to this fruity bar. You can make Peach-Apricot-Oat Squares by substituting ½ cup peach preserves for the strawberry preserves.

1 Serving: Calories 160 (Calories from Fat 40); Total Fat 4.5g (Saturated Fat 0.5g; Trans Fat 0g); Cholesterol 15mg; Sodium 105mg; Total Carbohydrate 27g (Dietary Fiber 2g; Sugars 17g); Protein 2g **% Daily Value:** Vitamin A 4%; Vitamin C 0%; Calcium 2%; Iron 4% **Exchanges:** ½ Starch, 1½ Other Carbohydrate, 1 Fat **Carbohydrate Choices:** 2

Crimson Crumble Bars

PREP TIME: **20 MINUTES** • START TO FINISH: **1 HOUR 55 MINUTES** • **36 BARS** • WHOLE GRAIN SERVING: ½

2 cups fresh or frozen
   cranberries

1 cup granulated sugar

2 teaspoons cornstarch

1 can (8 oz) crushed pineapple
   in unsweetened juice,
   undrained

1 cup whole wheat or
   all-purpose flour

2 cups old-fashioned oats

⅔ cup packed brown sugar

¼ teaspoon salt

¾ cup butter or margarine,
   cut into pieces

½ cup chopped pecans,
   if desired

1 Heat oven to 350°F. Spray 13 × 9-inch pan with cooking spray. In 2-quart saucepan, mix cranberries, granulated sugar, cornstarch and pineapple. Heat to boiling, stirring frequently; reduce heat. Cover; simmer 10 to 15 minutes, stirring occasionally, until cranberries pop and sauce is translucent.

2 Meanwhile, in large bowl, mix flour, oats, brown sugar and salt. Cut in butter, using pastry blender or fork, until crumbly. Stir in pecans. Reserve 1 cup mixture for topping. Press remaining crumb mixture in pan.

3 Pour fruit mixture over crust. Sprinkle with reserved crumb mixture.

4 Bake 28 to 32 minutes or until top is golden brown. Cool completely on cooling rack, at least 1 hour. For bars, cut into 6 rows by 6 rows.

Betty Tip

Packages of cranberries freeze well in their original plastic bags and don't even need to be thawed before using. Whole wheat flour adds an extra hit of whole grain to this good-to-the-last-crumb bar.

1 Bar: Calories 110 (Calories from Fat 40); Total Fat 4g (Saturated Fat 2.5g; Trans Fat 0g); Cholesterol 10mg; Sodium 45mg; Total Carbohydrate 17g (Dietary Fiber 1g; Sugars 11g); Protein 1g
% Daily Value: Vitamin A 2%; Vitamin C 0%; Calcium 0%; Iron 2%   **Exchanges:** ½ Starch, ½ Other Carbohydrate, 1 Fat   **Carbohydrate Choices:** 1

Chewy Barley-Nut Cookies

PREP TIME: **45 MINUTES** • START TO FINISH: **45 MINUTES** • **2 DOZEN COOKIES** • WHOLE GRAIN SERVING: **½**

⅓ cup canola oil

½ cup granulated sugar

¼ cup packed brown sugar

¼ reduced-fat mayonnaise or salad dressing

1 teaspoon vanilla

1 egg

2 cups rolled barley or 2 cups plus 2 tablespoons old-fashioned oats

¾ cup whole wheat flour

½ teaspoon baking soda

½ teaspoon salt

¼ teaspoon ground cinnamon

⅓ cup "heart-healthy" mixed nuts (peanuts, almonds, pistachios, pecans and hazelnuts)

1   Heat oven to 350°F. Spray cookie sheet with cooking spray.

2   In medium bowl, mix oil, sugars, mayonnaise, vanilla and egg with spoon. Stir in barley, flour, baking soda, salt and cinnamon. Stir in nuts.

3   Drop dough by measuring rounded tablespoonfuls 2 inches onto cookie sheet.

4   Bake 10 to 14 minutes or until edges are golden brown. Cool 2 minutes; remove from cookie sheet to cooling rack.

Betty Tip

If you haven't seen rolled barley, look for it at your favorite co-op or health food store. It works well in place of old-fashioned oats (also called rolled oats) in many recipes.

1 Cookie: Calories 150 (Calories from Fat 50); Total Fat 5g (Saturated Fat 0.5g; Trans Fat 0g); Cholesterol 10mg; Sodium 100mg; Total Carbohydrate 23g (Dietary Fiber 3g; Sugars 7g); Protein 3g **% Daily Value:** Vitamin A 0%; Vitamin C 0%; Calcium 0%; Iron 4% **Exchanges:** 1 Starch, ½ Other Carbohydrate, 1 Fat **Carbohydrate Choices:** 1½

Cranberry-Orange Oatmeal Cookies

PREP TIME: **35 MINUTES** • START TO FINISH: **35 MINUTES** • **2 DOZEN COOKIES** • WHOLE GRAIN SERVING: **½**

½ cup canola oil

½ cup granulated sugar

¼ cup packed brown sugar

1 teaspoon vanilla

2 eggs

2 cups old-fashioned or
quick-cooking oats

⅔ cup whole wheat flour

1 teaspoon ground ginger

½ teaspoon ground allspice

½ teaspoon baking soda

¼ teaspoon salt

½ cup orange-flavored dried
cranberries

¼ cup chopped walnuts

1 Heat oven to 350°F. In large bowl, mix oil, sugars, vanilla and eggs with spoon. Stir in oats, flour, ginger, allspice, baking soda and salt. Stir in cranberries and walnuts.

2 Onto ungreased cookie sheet, drop dough by tablespoonfuls 2 inches apart.

3 Bake 11 to 14 minutes or until edges turn golden brown. Cool 1 minute; remove from cookie sheet to cooling rack.

Betty Tip

The oats replace some of the flour to make this a chewy, nutty and very yummy cookie. The orange flavor added to the cranberries is terrific with the spices.

1 Cookie: Calories 130 (Calories from Fat 60); Total Fat 6g (Saturated Fat 0.5g; Trans Fat 0g); Cholesterol 20mg; Sodium 55mg; Total Carbohydrate 16g (Dietary Fiber 1g; Sugars 8g); Protein 2g **% Daily Value:** Vitamin A 0%; Vitamin C 0%; Calcium 0%; Iron 4% **Exchanges:** ½ Starch, ½ Other Carbohydrate, 1 Fat **Carbohydrate Choices:** 1

Ranger Cookies

PREP TIME: **15 MINUTES** • START TO FINISH: **1 HOUR 15 MINUTES** • **ABOUT 4½ DOZEN COOKIES** •
WHOLE GRAIN SERVING: ½

2 cups packed brown sugar

1 cup butter or margarine, softened

1 teaspoon vanilla

2 eggs

2 cups whole wheat flour

2 cups old-fashioned or quick-cooking oats

1 teaspoon baking powder

1 teaspoon baking soda

1½ cups Wheaties® cereal

1 cup salted peanuts

1 Heat oven to 350°F. In large bowl, mix brown sugar, butter, vanilla and eggs with spoon. Stir in flour, oats, baking powder and baking soda. Stir in cereal and peanuts.

2 Shape dough by rounded teaspoonfuls into balls. On ungreased cookie sheet, place balls about 2 inches apart. Flatten slightly with greased bottom of glass dipped into sugar.

3 Bake 10 to 12 minutes or until set. Cool 1 minute; remove from cookie sheet to cooling rack.

Betty Tip

If you bake cookies often, having several cookie sheets is convenient. As one sheet of cookies is baking, you can get another one ready to go. Let the cookie sheets cool a few minutes between bakings or the cookie dough will start to spread before it's placed in the oven.

1 Cookie: Calories 110 (Calories from Fat 45); Total Fat 5g (Saturated Fat 2.5g; Trans Fat 0g); Cholesterol 15mg; Sodium 90mg; Total Carbohydrate 15g (Dietary Fiber 1g; Sugars 8g); Protein 2g **% Daily Value:** Vitamin A 2%; Vitamin C 0%; Calcium 0%; Iron 4% **Exchanges:** ½ Starch, ½ Other Carbohydrate, 1 Fat **Carbohydrate Choices:** 1

Giant Oat Cookies

PREP TIME: **1 HOUR** • START TO FINISH: **1 HOUR** • **12 LARGE COOKIES** • WHOLE GRAIN SERVING: ½

¼ cup butter or margarine,
   softened

1½ cups sugar

⅓ cup canola oil

1 teaspoon vanilla

2 eggs

1½ cups all-purpose flour

1 cup old-fashioned or
   quick-cooking oats

1 teaspoon baking soda

½ teaspoon salt

3 cups Cheerios® cereal

1 Heat oven to 375°F. In large bowl, beat butter and sugar with electric mixer on medium speed until blended. Beat in oil, vanilla and eggs until well mixed. On low speed, beat in flour, oats, baking soda and salt until dough forms. Stir in cereal.

2 For each cookie, roll ⅓ cup of the dough into a ball. Place balls 2 inches apart on 2 ungreased cookie sheets.

3 Bake 9 to 11 minutes or until light brown. Cool 2 minutes; remove from cookie sheets to cooling rack. Cool completely, about 20 minutes. Store in tightly covered container.

Betty Tip

Though it may be difficult to wait, letting these cookies cool a few minutes before removing them from the cookie sheets ensures that they will hold together.

1 Large Cookie: Calories 310 (Calories from Fat 110); Total Fat 12g (Saturated Fat 3g; Trans Fat 0g); Cholesterol 45mg; Sodium 290mg; Total Carbohydrate 47g (Dietary Fiber 2g; Sugars 26g); Protein 5g **% Daily Value:** Vitamin A 6%; Vitamin C 0%; Calcium 4%; Iron 15% **Exchanges:** 1 Starch, 2 Other Carbohydrate, 2½ Fat **Carbohydrate Choices:** 3

Gingerbread with Lemon Topping

PREP TIME: **15 MINUTES** • START TO FINISH: **1 HOUR 10 MINUTES** • **8 SERVINGS** • WHOLE GRAIN SERVING: ½

Gingerbread

1 cup all-purpose flour

1 cup whole wheat flour

½ cup mild-flavor (light) or full-flavor (dark) molasses

½ cup hot water

¼ cup packed brown sugar

¼ cup butter or margarine, softened

1 teaspoon baking soda

1 teaspoon ground ginger

1 teaspoon ground cinnamon

¼ teaspoon salt

1 egg

Lemon Sauce

3 tablespoons granulated sugar

1 tablespoon cornstarch

1¼ cups water

1 egg yolk, beaten

1 tablespoon grated lemon peel

2 tablespoons lemon juice

1 Heat oven to 325°F. Spray 9 × 5-inch or 8 × 4-inch loaf pan with cooking spray. In medium bowl, beat all gingerbread ingredients with electric mixer on low speed 30 seconds, scraping bowl constantly. Beat on medium speed 1 to 2 minutes, scraping bowl occasionally, until well mixed. Pour into pan.

2 Bake 40 to 45 minutes or until toothpick inserted in center comes out clean.

3 Meanwhile, in 1-quart saucepan, mix granulated sugar and cornstarch. Gradually stir in 1¼ cups water. Cook over medium heat, stirring constantly, until mixture thickens and boils. Stir in egg yolk. Boil and stir 1 minute; remove from heat. Stir in lemon peel and lemon juice.

4 Cool gingerbread 10 minutes; remove from pan. Serve warm or cool gingerbread with warm or cool lemon sauce.

Betty Tip

Want to give gingerbread a strong, spicy flavor? Use dark molasses. Or for a sweeter, more delicately flavored cake, use light molasses. The lemon sauce and ginger create a light, flavorful cake and sauce.

1 Serving: Calories 300 (Calories from Fat 70); Total Fat 8g (Saturated Fat 2g; Trans Fat 1g); Cholesterol 50mg; Sodium 250mg; Total Carbohydrate 52g (Dietary Fiber 3g; Sugars 23g); Protein 5g **% Daily Value:** Vitamin A 0%; Vitamin C 0%; Calcium 6%; Iron 15% **Exchanges:** 1½ Starch, 2 Other Carbohydrate, 1½ Fat **Carbohydrate Choices:** 3½

Oatmeal Brownies

PREP TIME: **15 MINUTES** • START TO FINISH: **3 HOURS 10 MINUTES** • **40 BROWNIES** • WHOLE GRAIN SERVING: ½

2½ cups old-fashioned or quick-cooking oats

¾ cup whole wheat or all-purpose flour

¾ cup packed brown sugar

½ teaspoon baking soda

¾ cup butter or margarine, melted

1 box (1 lb 2.4 oz) supreme brownie mix with pouch of chocolate flavor syrup

¼ cup water

¼ cup canola oil

1 or 2 eggs

½ cup chopped nuts, if desired

1 Heat oven to 350°F (325°F for dark or nonstick pan). Grease bottom only of 13 × 9-inch pan with shortening or cooking spray.

2 In medium bowl, mix oats, flour, brown sugar and baking soda; stir in butter. Reserve 1 cup of the oat mixture. Press remaining oat mixture in pan. Bake 10 minutes; cool 5 minutes.

3 In medium bowl, stir brownie mix, chocolate syrup, water, oil and 1 egg for fudgelike brownies (or 2 eggs for cakelike brownies) until well blended. Stir in nuts. Spread over baked layer; sprinkle with reserved oat mixture.

4 Bake 40 to 45 minutes or until toothpick inserted 2 inches from side of pan comes out clean or almost clean. Cool completely, about 2 hours. For brownies, cut into 8 rows by 5 rows. Store tightly covered.

Betty Tip

Use old-fashioned (rolled) oats often in your baking. Not only do they add flavor and texture to baked goods, but they are also 100 percent whole grain.

1 Brownie: Calories 150 (Calories from Fat 60); Total Fat 7g (Saturated Fat 3g; Trans Fat 0g); Cholesterol 15mg; Sodium 85mg; Total Carbohydrate 20g (Dietary Fiber 1g; Sugars 15g); Protein 1g **% Daily Value:** Vitamin A 2%; Vitamin C 0%; Calcium 0%; Iron 4% **Exchanges:** ½ Starch, 1 Other Carbohydrate, 1 Fat **Carbohydrate Choices:** 1

Crunch-Topped Apple-Spice Cake

PREP TIME: **20 MINUTES** • START TO FINISH: **2 HOURS 5 MINUTES** • **15 SERVINGS** • WHOLE GRAIN SERVING: ½

⅓ cup boiling water

2 medium unpeeled cooking apples, chopped (2 cups)

1¼ cups packed brown sugar

1 cup all-purpose flour

1 cup whole wheat flour

⅓ cup canola oil

1 teaspoon baking soda

1 teaspoon ground cinnamon

1 teaspoon vanilla

½ teaspoon ground cloves

¼ teaspoon salt

3 eggs

⅓ cup finely chopped nuts

2 tablespoons packed brown sugar

1   Heat oven to 350°F. Spray 13 × 9-inch pan with cooking spray; sprinkle with flour.

2   In large bowl, pour boiling water over apples. Add remaining ingredients except nuts and brown sugar. Beat with electric mixer on low speed 1 minute, scraping bowl constantly. Beat on medium speed 2 minutes, scraping bowl occasionally. Pour into pan.

3   In small bowl, mix nuts and brown sugar; sprinkle over batter.

4   Bake 40 to 45 minutes or until toothpick inserted in center comes out clean. Cool completely, about 1 hour.

Betty Tip

Many traditional recipes for apple cake call for the nuts to be stirred into the batter. By replacing a larger amount of stirred-in nuts with the nut topping in this recipe, you'll get maximum flavor with a lot less fat.

1 Serving: Calories 230 (Calories from Fat 70); Total Fat 8g (Saturated Fat 1g; Trans Fat 0g); Cholesterol 40mg; Sodium 140mg; Total Carbohydrate 35g (Dietary Fiber 2g; Sugars 21g); Protein 4g
% Daily Value: Vitamin A 0%; Vitamin C 0%; Calcium 4%; Iron 8% **Exchanges:** 1 Starch, 1½ Other Carbohydrate, 1½ Fat **Carbohydrate Choices:** 2

Double Chocolate–Kasha Torte

PREP TIME: **25 MINUTES** • START TO FINISH: **1 HOUR 25 MINUTES** • **10 SERVINGS** • WHOLE GRAIN SERVING: ½

½ cup boiling water

½ cup uncooked roasted buckwheat kernels or groats (kasha)

½ cup semisweet chocolate chips

¼ cup butter or margarine, softened

¾ cup whole wheat flour

2 tablespoons unsweetened baking cocoa

1 teaspoon baking powder

¼ teaspoon salt

⅓ cup packed brown sugar

⅓ cup granulated sugar

½ teaspoon vanilla

1 egg

3 cups sliced fresh strawberries

2 tablespoons granulated sugar

2 teaspoons powdered sugar

Betty Tip

Kasha, a whole grain, and buckwheat groats are one and the same thing. In this tasty torte, the roasted kasha lends a nutty texture and flavor, with a lot less fat than nuts would add. Enjoy!

1   Heat oven to 350°F. Line bottom of 9-inch springform pan with cooking parchment paper.

2   In medium bowl, pour boiling water over kasha, chocolate chips and butter; let stand 15 minutes.

3   Meanwhile, in another medium bowl, mix flour, cocoa, baking powder and salt; set aside.

4   In large bowl, beat brown sugar, ⅓ cup granulated sugar, the vanilla and egg with electric mixer on low speed about 1 minute or until blended. Stir kasha mixture to combine; add to sugar mixture and stir to blend. Add flour mixture; beat on low speed about 2 minutes or until blended. Spread batter in pan.

5   Bake 30 to 35 minutes until center is set and toothpick inserted 1 inch from edge comes out clean.

6   Cool torte in pan 20 minutes. Meanwhile, in medium bowl, mix strawberries and 2 tablespoons granulated sugar. Let stand 15 to 20 minutes.

7   Remove side of springform pan. Place cooling rack upside down on torte; turn rack and torte over. Remove bottom of pan and parchment paper. Place plate upside down on torte; turn plate and rack over. Remove rack from top of torte.

8   To serve, sprinkle powdered sugar over top of torte. Spoon about ⅓ cup strawberries over each serving.

1 Serving: Calories 240 (Calories from Fat 70); Total Fat 8g (Saturated Fat 4.5g; Trans Fat 0g); Cholesterol 35mg; Sodium 150mg; Total Carbohydrate 37g (Dietary Fiber 4g; Sugars 24g); Protein 3g
% Daily Value: Vitamin A 4%; Vitamin C 50%; Calcium 6%; Iron 8%   **Exchanges:** 1 Starch, ½ Fruit, 1 Other Carbohydrate, 1½ Fat   **Carbohydrate Choices:** 2½

Frozen Strawberry Cheesecake

PREP TIME: **25 MINUTES** • START TO FINISH: **6 HOURS 15 MINUTES** • **9 SERVINGS** • WHOLE GRAIN SERVING: ¼

Crust

2 tablespoons butter or
    margarine, melted

½ cup old-fashioned oats

¼ cup finely chopped walnuts

3 tablespoons ground flaxseed
    or flaxseed meal

2 tablespoons shredded
    coconut

2 tablespoons whole wheat
    flour

⅛ teaspoon ground cinnamon

Dash salt

Filling

1 box (3.4 oz) instant
    cheesecake pudding and
    pie filling mix

1 cup milk

2 cups vanilla reduced-fat ice
    cream, softened

1 cup chopped fresh
    strawberries (5 oz)

1 pint (2 cups) strawberry
    sorbet, softened

5 fresh strawberries, cut in half,
    if desired

1 Heat oven to 350°F. In medium bowl, mix all crust ingredients. Press in bottom and up side of 9-inch glass pie plate. Bake about 10 minutes or until golden brown. Cool completely, about 30 minutes.

2 In large bowl, beat pudding mix and milk with wire whisk until smooth. Gently stir in ice cream with wire whisk until smooth. Stir in chopped strawberries. Pour mixture into cooled crust. Freeze 2 to 3 hours or until firm.

3 Spread sorbet evenly over ice cream. Freeze 2 hours.

4 Remove from freezer 10 minutes before serving. Cut into wedges. Garnish each wedge with strawberry half.

Betty Tip

You'll be asked for the recipe for this stunning dessert. Gladly hand it over—coconut, strawberries and sorbet added to flaxseed, whole-grain oats and walnuts is a wonderful combination of flavors and textures.

1 Serving: Calories 270 (Calories from Fat 80); Total Fat 9g (Saturated Fat 4g; Trans Fat 0g); Cholesterol 20mg; Sodium 240mg; Total Carbohydrate 42g (Dietary Fiber 2g; Sugars 30g); Protein 4g **% Daily Value:** Vitamin A 6%; Vitamin C 20%; Calcium 8%; Iron 4% **Exchanges:** 1 Starch, 2 Other Carbohydrate, 1½ Fat **Carbohydrate Choices:** 3

Apple-Cinnamon-Raisin Bread Pudding

PREP TIME: **20 MINUTES** • START TO FINISH: **1 HOUR 40 MINUTES** • **12 SERVINGS** • WHOLE GRAIN SERVING: ½

Bread Pudding

6 cups cubed 100% whole
  wheat bread (8 slices)

½ cup raisins

2 medium apples, peeled,
  thinly sliced (2 cups)

4 eggs

¾ cup granulated sugar

1 teaspoon ground cinnamon

¼ teaspoon salt

3 cups milk

1 teaspoon vanilla

Streusel Topping

¾ cup all-purpose flour

½ cup old-fashioned oats

½ cup packed brown sugar

1 teaspoon ground cinnamon

¼ cup butter or margarine,
  melted

1 Heat oven to 350°F. In ungreased 13 × 9-inch (3-quart) glass baking dish, toss bread, raisins and apples.

2 In large bowl, beat eggs, granulated sugar, 1 teaspoon cinnamon and the salt with wire whisk until well blended. Beat in milk and vanilla. Pour milk mixture over bread mixture. Let stand 5 minutes.

3 Meanwhile, in small bowl, mix all topping ingredients; sprinkle evenly over unbaked pudding.

4 Bake 40 to 50 minutes or until center is puffed and golden. Cool at least 30 minutes.

Betty Tip

Using whole wheat bread in this traditional bread pudding adds several grams of whole grain. To get three servings of whole grain daily, make choices that will increase your servings of whole grain, even in your desserts.

1 Serving: Calories 300 (Calories from Fat 70); Total Fat 8g (Saturated Fat 4g; Trans Fat 0g); Cholesterol 85mg; Sodium 230mg; Total Carbohydrate 50g (Dietary Fiber 3g; Sugars 32g); Protein 8g **% Daily Value:** Vitamin A 6%; Vitamin C 0%; Calcium 10%; Iron 10% **Exchanges:** 1 Starch, 2 Other Carbohydrate, ½ Low-Fat Milk, 1 Fat **Carbohydrate Choices:** 3

grains glossary

Amaranth: Tiny seeds of the amaranth plant that, when cooked, resemble brown caviar. Amaranth is high in protein and is gluten-free. It's used in breads, muffins, crackers and pancakes, but it can be rather hard to find.

Amaranth

Barley: One of the oldest cultivated grains, barley has a tough hull that's difficult to remove without taking off some of the bran. Hulled barley, available at health-food stores and through Internet sources, retains more of the whole-grain nutrients but takes longer to cook and is harder to find. Pearled barley has some of the bran removed, so is not technically a whole grain. The fiber in barley is especially healthy because it may help lower cholesterol. **Rolled barley flakes** are similar in appearance to rolled oats and can be substituted for old-fashioned oats.

Quick-Cooking Barley: Pearled barley that has been cooked and dried; cooks in about 10 minutes but is not a whole grain because the bran has been removed.

Brown Rice: Whole-grain rice is usually brown but can be black, purple, red or other hues. Brown basmati rice is also a whole grain. Rice thrives in warm, humid climates. In the United States, rice is grown in Arkansas, California, Louisiana, Mississippi, Missouri and Texas.

Buckwheat: High in protein, buckwheat also contains B vitamins and is rich in phosphorus, potassium, iron and calcium. Also known as buckwheat contains no gluten, so it's ideal for people who struggle with wheat allergies and cannot tolerate gluten.

Buckwheat Flour: This is often used for making buckwheat pancakes and other baked goods.

Corn: A very common grain, the whole kernels are ground into whole-grain **cornmeal**, which is used in baking cornbread, corn muffins, etc. In New Mexico, a primary place to grow corn, you can find red, white, blue and yellow corn. **Popcorn**, a slightly different strain of corn grown in the Midwest, is also a whole grain.

Kamut®: An ancient grain originally grown in Egypt, it is the trademarked name of a grain grown on organic farms primarily in Montana. The kernels look like wheat kernels but are lighter brown and larger.

Millet: Often found in birdseed in the United States, it's the leading staple grain in India and is commonly eaten in China, South America, Russia and the Himalayas. Millet is a small, round, ivory grain with a mild flavor that mixes well with other foods and tastes great toasted.

Oats: Because the bran and germ are still intact in old-fashioned and quick-cooking oats, both are considered a whole grain. Steel-cut oats, also called or , are chewier and nuttier. The fiber in oats is especially healthy because it may help lower cholesterol.

Quinoa: Pronounced "KEEN-wa," is native to South America, where it is grown in high altitudes. A small, light-colored, round grain, quinoa cooks in about 10 to 12 minutes and makes a light, fluffy side dish. It can also be used in soups and salads.

Rye: A hardy, fibrous grain, rye is widely grown in northern Europe, where the weather gets extremely cold. Rye is best known for the deep, rich flavor that it adds to breads. It's available as rye flour and rye berries. Look for rye

Rye field

berries in co-ops and health-food stores or on the Internet. **Rolled rye flakes**, which is rolled rye that is similar in appearance to rolled oats, can be substituted for old-fashioned oats.

Sorghum: Also called sorghum originated in Africa and can be popped and eaten as a snack, cooked into porridge or ground into flour for baked goods. Sorghum, a gluten-free grain, can be hard to find.

Spelt: A variety of wheat, spelt has a nutty flavor and is higher in protein than regular wheat. Used as an ingredient in pasta and other products in the supermarket, the grain itself can be hard to find.

Teff: This tiny grain is used in Ethiopia to make the spongy flatbread Teff has a sweet, molasses-like flavor and comes in three colors (red, brown and white). All colors are whole grains because the grain is too tiny to mill. Teff is not very available in the United States.

Triticale: A hybrid of wheat and rye, this modified grain makes great

Sorghum

breads. Most of this grain is grown in Europe and can be hard to find in the United States.

Wheat Berries: The world's largest crop, these are the whole kernels of hard red spring wheat. Chewy and nutty, they can be cooked and served as a main or side dish. **Whole wheat flakes**, rolled wheat that is similar in appearance to rolled oats, can be substituted for old-fashioned oats.

Bulgur Wheat: Wheat kernels that are boiled, dried and cracked. Because

bulgur has been precooked, it takes only 20 minutes to cook. Best known as the ingredient in Middle Eastern it's sometimes referred to as the Middle Eastern pasta.

Cracked Wheat: Wheat kernels that have been cracked and split open, they cook much more quickly than wheat berries. Cracked wheat is also used as an ingredient in breads.

Whole Wheat Flour: The whole kernel is ground so it contains the bran, endosperm and germ. It can be used in combination with all-purpose flour (or substituted for all-purpose flour, if you are used to the flavor and appearance) in pancakes, waffles, breads and cookies.

Wild Rice: The seed of an aquatic grass originally grown around the Great Lakes in the United States. Wild rice has twice the protein and fiber of brown rice, but it has less iron and calcium. Wild rice is more expensive than many other grains, but it's usually widely available. Its hardy flavor and dark color make it an ideal ingredient in soups, stews and casseroles.

helpful nutrition and cooking information

Nutrition Guidelines

We provide nutrition information for each recipe that includes calories, fat, cholesterol, sodium, carbohydrate, fiber and protein. Individual food choices can be based on this information.

Recommended intake for a daily diet of 2,000 calories as set by the Food and Drug Administration

Total Fat	Less than 65g
Saturated Fat	Less than 20g
Cholesterol	Less than 300mg
Sodium	Less than 2,400mg
Total Carbohydrate	300g
Dietary Fiber	25g

Criteria Used for Calculating Nutrition Information

- The first ingredient was used wherever a choice is given (such as ⅓ cup sour cream or plain yogurt).

- The first ingredient amount was used wherever a range is given (such as 3- to 3-½–pound cut-up broiler-fryer chicken).

- The first serving number was used wherever a range is given (such as 4 to 6 servings).

- "If desired" ingredients and recipe variations were not included (such as sprinkle with brown sugar, if desired).

- Only the amount of a marinade or frying oil that is estimated to be absorbed by the food during preparation or cooking was calculated.

Ingredients Used in Recipe Testing and Nutrition Calculations

- Ingredients used for testing represent those that the majority of consumers use in their homes: large eggs, 2% milk, 80%-lean ground beef, canned ready-to-use chicken broth and vegetable oil spread containing not less than 65 percent fat.

- Fat-free, low-fat or low-sodium products were not used, unless otherwise indicated.

- Solid vegetable shortening (not butter, margarine, nonstick cooking sprays or vegetable oil spread as they can cause sticking problems) was used to grease pans, unless otherwise indicated.

Equipment Used in Recipe Testing

We use equipment for testing that the majority of consumers use in their homes. If a specific piece of equipment (such as a wire whisk) is necessary for recipe success, it is listed in the recipe.

- Cookware and bakeware without nonstick coatings were used, unless otherwise indicated.

- No dark-colored, black or insulated bakeware was used.

- When a pan is specified in a recipe, a metal pan was used; a baking dish or pie plate means ovenproof glass was used.

- An electric hand mixer was used for mixing only when mixer speeds are specified in the recipe directions. When a mixer speed is not given, a spoon or fork was used.

Cooking Terms Glossary

Beat: Mix ingredients vigorously with spoon, fork, wire whisk, hand beater or electric mixer until smooth and uniform.

Boil: Heat liquid until bubbles rise continuously and break on the surface and steam is given off. For rolling boil, the bubbles form rapidly.

Chop: Cut into coarse or fine irregular pieces with a knife, food chopper, blender or food processor.

Cube: Cut into squares $\frac{1}{2}$ inch or larger.

Dice: Cut into squares smaller than $\frac{1}{2}$ inch.

Grate: Cut into tiny particles using small rough holes of grater (citrus peel or chocolate).

Grease: Rub the inside surface of a pan with shortening, using pastry brush, piece of waxed paper or paper towel, to prevent food from sticking during baking (as for some casseroles).

Julienne: Cut into thin, matchlike strips, using knife or food processor (vegetables, fruits and meats).

Mix: Combine ingredients in any way that distributes them evenly.

Sauté: Cook foods in hot oil or margarine over medium-high heat with frequent tossing and turning motion.

Shred: Cut into long, thin pieces by rubbing food across the holes of a shredder, as for cheese, or by using a knife to slice very thinly, as for cabbage.

Simmer: Cook in liquid just below the boiling point on top of the stove; usually after reducing heat from a boil. Bubbles will rise slowly and break just below the surface.

Stir: Mix ingredients until uniform consistency. Stir once in a while for stirring occasionally, often for stirring frequently and continuously for stirring constantly.

Toss: Tumble ingredients (such as green salad) lightly with a lifting motion, usually to coat evenly or mix with another food.

metric conversion guide

VOLUME

U.S. UNITS	CANADIAN METRIC	AUSTRALIAN METRIC
¼ teaspoon	1 mL	1 ml
½ teaspoon	2 mL	2 ml
1 teaspoon	5 mL	5 ml
1 tablespoon	15 mL	20 ml
¼ cup	50 mL	60 ml
⅓ cup	75 mL	80 ml
½ cup	125 mL	125 ml
⅔ cup	150 mL	170 ml
¾ cup	175 mL	190 ml
1 cup	250 mL	250 ml
1 quart	1 liter	1 liter
1½ quarts	1.5 liters	1.5 liters
2 quarts	2 liters	2 liters
2½ quarts	2.5 liters	2.5 liters
3 quarts	3 liters	3 liters
4 quarts	4 liters	4 liters

WEIGHT

U.S. UNITS	CANADIAN METRIC	AUSTRALIAN METRIC
1 ounce	30 grams	30 grams
2 ounces	55 grams	60 grams
3 ounces	85 grams	90 grams
4 ounces (¼ pound)	115 grams	125 grams
8 ounces (½ pound)	225 grams	225 grams
16 ounces (1 pound)	455 grams	500 grams
1 pound	455 grams	½ kilogram

MEASUREMENTS

INCHES	CENTIMETERS
1	2.5
2	5.0
3	7.5
4	10.0
5	12.5
6	15.0
7	17.5
8	20.5
9	23.0
10	25.5
11	28.0
12	30.5
13	33.0

TEMPERATURES

FAHRENHEIT	CELSIUS
32°	0°
212°	100°
250°	120°
275°	140°
300°	150°
325°	160°
350°	180°
375°	190°
400°	200°
425°	220°
450°	230°
475°	240°
500°	260°

NOTE: The recipes in this cookbook have not been developed or tested using metric measures. When converting recipes to metric, some variations in quality may be noted.

index

Note: *Italicized* page references indicate photographs.

Complete your cookbook library with these *Betty Crocker* titles

Betty Crocker 30-Minute Meals for Diabetes

Betty Crocker 300 Calorie Cookbook

Betty Crocker Baking Basics

Betty Crocker Baking for Today

Betty Crocker's Best Bread Machine Cookbook

Betty Crocker's Best-Loved Recipes

Betty Crocker The Big Book of Cookies

Betty Crocker The Big Book of Cupcakes

Betty Crocker The Big Book of Slow Cooker, Casseroles & More

Betty Crocker The Big Book of Weeknight Dinners

Betty Crocker Bisquick® II Cookbook

Betty Crocker Bisquick® Impossibly Easy Pies

Betty Crocker Bisquick® to the Rescue

Betty Crocker Christmas Cookbook

Betty Crocker's Cook Book for Boys and Girls

Betty Crocker Cookbook, 11th Edition— *The* **BIG RED** *Cookbook*®

Betty Crocker Cookbook, Bridal Edition

Betty Crocker's Cooking Basics

Betty Crocker's Cooky Book, Facsimile Edition

Betty Crocker Country Cooking

Betty Crocker Decorating Cakes and Cupcakes

Betty Crocker's Diabetes Cookbook

Betty Crocker's Easy Slow Cooker Dinners

Betty Crocker's Eat and Lose Weight

Betty Crocker Fix-with-a-Mix Desserts

Betty Crocker Gluten-Free Cooking

Betty Crocker Grilling Made Easy

Betty Crocker Healthy Heart Cookbook

Betty Crocker's Indian Home Cooking

Betty Crocker's Italian Cooking

Betty Crocker's Kids Cook!

Betty Crocker Living with Cancer Cookbook

Betty Crocker Low-Carb Lifestyle Cookbook

Betty Crocker's Low-Fat, Low-Cholesterol Cooking Today

Betty Crocker Money Saving Meals

Betty Crocker More Slow Cooker Recipes

Betty Crocker's New Cake Decorating

Betty Crocker One-Dish Meals

Betty Crocker's Picture Cook Book, Facsimile Edition

Betty Crocker's Quick & Easy Cookbook

Betty Crocker's Slow Cooker Cookbook

Betty Crocker Ultimate Bisquick® Cookbook

Betty Crocker's Ultimate Cake Mix Cookbook

Betty Crocker's Vegetarian Cooking

Betty Crocker Why It Works